Helion & Company Limited
Unit 8 Amherst Business Centre
Budbrooke Road
Warwick
CV34 5WE
England
Tel. 01926 499 619
Email: info@helion.co.uk
Website: www.helion.co.uk
Twitter: @helionbooks
Visit our blog http://blog.helion.co.uk/

Text © Bojan Dimitrijević 2023
Photographs © as individually credited
Colour artwork © David Bocquelet, Tom
    Cooper, Peter Penev 2023

Designed and typeset by Farr out
    Publications, Wokingham, Berkshire
Cover design Paul Hewitt, Battlefield Design
    (www.battlefield-design.co.uk)

Every reasonable effort has been made to
trace copyright holders and to obtain their
permission for the use of copyright material.
The author and publisher apologise for any
errors or omissions in this work, and would
be grateful if notified of any corrections that
should be incorporated in future reprints or
editions of this book.

ISBN 978-1-804510-28-5

British Library Cataloguing-in-Publication
    Data
A catalogue record for this book is available
    from the British Library

We always welcome receiving book
proposals from prospective authors.

CONTENTS

MAP OF EUROPE 1945–1992

Note: In order to simplify the use of this book, all names, locations and geographic
designations are as provided in *The Times World Atlas*, or other traditionally accepted major
sources of reference, as of the time of described events.

ACKNOWLEDGEMENTS

For the photographs used in this volume, the author wishes to thank: the Media Centre of the Serbian Ministry of Defence and its chief, Radovan Popović and its main photographer, Zoran Milovanovic, for their assistance in researching illustrations; my very dear friend Milan Micevski for mutual work on the history of the Yugoslav Air Force in the Cold War; the families of Aleksandar Ranković, General Nikola Maravic and Colonel Ladislav Žanović; and the Museum of Yugoslavia – especially, senior curator Radovan Cukic; as well the family of Rista Marjanovic, the famous Serbian photographer and his granddaughter, Zorana, for colour photos taken in 1945.

Finally, I am very grateful to my editor, Tom Cooper, the kind members of the Helion staff who were engaged in the preparation of this material and of course, publisher Duncan Rogers for his confidence and support.

ABBREVIATIONS

AA	Anti-aircraft
AFB	Air Force Base
AJ	*Arhiv Jugoslavije* (Archive of Yugoslavia)
AMAS	American Military Assistance Staff
AVH	*Államvédelmi Hatóság* (State Protection Authority)
CIA	Central Intelligence Agency
HQ	Headquarters
JA	*Jugoslovenska armija* (Yugoslav Army)
JNA	*Jugoslovenska narodna armija* (Yugoslav People's Army)
JRM	*Jugoslovenska ratna mornarica* (Yugoslav Navy)
KOS	*Kontraobaveštajna sluzba* (Counterintelligence Service)
KNOJ	*Korpus narodne odbrane Jugoslavije* (Yugoslav People's Defence Corps)
KPJ	*Komunistička Partija Jugoslavije* (Communist Party of Yugoslavia)
MAP	Military Assistance Pact
MDAP	Mutual Defence Aid Programme
MNO	*Ministarstvo narodne odbrane* or Ministry of National Defence (MoD)
NATO	North Atlantic Treaty Organization
NCO	Non-Commissioned Officer
NKVD	*Naródnyi Komissariát Vnútrennikh Del* (The People's Commissariat for Internal Affairs) Soviet Security Service
OZNA	*Odeljenje za zaštitu naroda* (Section for Protection of People)
POW	Prisoner of War
RAF	Royal Air Force
SSR	Soviet Socialist Republic
TAM	*Tvornica automobila Maribor* (Automobile Factory Maribor)
TDY	Temporary Duty
UDBA	*Uprava državne bezbednosti* (Department of State Security)
UNRRA	United Nations Relief and Rehabilitation Administration
US	United States
USAF	United States Air Force
USAAF	United States Army Air Force
USS	United States Ship
VA	*Vojni arhiv* (Military Archive)
VOC	*Vazduhoplovni opitni centar* (Aviation Test Centre)
VP	*vojna pošta* (Military post)
YAF	Yugoslav Air Force

INTRODUCTION

The Coniform Crisis that started in mid-1948 – the political, ideological and military conflict between Tito's Yugoslavia and the People's Democracy states led by the Soviet Union – was a significant event in the early Cold War in Europe. It began as a silent misunderstanding in 1944 and turned into a dispute between the Soviet and Yugoslav Communist Parties in the early days of 1948. This conflict became open and public later that year and then escalated into a small war until the period following Stalin's death in 1953.

This book starts with a short explanation of the 'Sovietisation' of the former Yugoslav Partisan Army, its ambitious developing plans and its influence in Albania, Bulgaria and the Greek Civil War leading to the rise of suspicion in Soviet leadership, especially Stalin. This resulted in a slow break up of mutual ties during the spring of 1948 and finally, in the Cominform Resolution on 28 June 1948.

The Resolution marked the start of the conflict that lasted for almost seven years. Communist brothers-in-arms became bitter enemies; Yugoslavian borders to the communist countries of Albania, Bulgaria, Romania and Hungary, almost became front lines.

In the military sense, the Crisis came somewhat out of the blue for both sides. Tito's Yugoslavs did not expect such levels of pressure from their ideological brothers nor from the idealised Stalin and the Soviet Union. On the other side, the Soviets counted on 'healthy forces' in the leadership of the Yugoslav Communist Party and did not assemble their troops for eventual intervention and the changing of Tito's leadership. As the Crisis slowly evolved into a small border war, the real war in the Korean peninsula changed the focus of major players on the world stage. Crisis and conflict at the Yugoslavian borders remained with the same tempo: border incidents, movement of troops, an intelligence war and propaganda efforts. It was an unusual but acute crisis: former hatreds between the Yugoslav nations and their neighbours – recently papered-over by new ideology and Soviet military presence – now exploded again. Red Stars were worn on both sides of the fence but the new ideology was interpreted in different ways.

The Cominform-Yugoslav conflict only ended because of external events. The first was the acceptance by Yugoslavia of the US Mutual Defence Aid Programme in November 1951 which led to Tito's Army being treated (almost) as one of the southern European NATO armies. Secondly, Stalin's death in March 1953, opened the possibility that the clashes could come to an end with Nikita Khrushchev's public declaration of a new policy of reconciliation in Belgrade in mid-1955. The actual military threat from the Soviet Army and the forces of the satellite states can still not be confirmed by the archival sources kept in Moscow.

The Cominform Crisis became the first crack in the emerging communist world in Europe which looked from the outside, to be monolithic. Inside the communist world, Yugoslavia proclaimed its own path into socialism/communism and managed to defend it. Outside in the West, the conflict was not registered as serious for almost two years. But then, it turned out to be perceived as a very important strategic shift in southeast Europe. The brick from the emerging communist wall was pulled out. Tito's Yugoslavia became an important military ally against the Soviets and their satellites. Moreover, it became a model for the other countries that remained under Soviet hegemony; how to lead a policy of 'socialism with human face' and be independent from Moscow.

As Bulgarian historian Roumen Daskalov suggests, conflict with Tito made Stalin aware of the dangers of 'separate paths to socialism' which led to a tightening of the socialist camp and an acceleration

of changes according to the Soviet model. So-called People's Democracy was replaced with the 'acceleration of the revolutionary process' and the 'dictatorship of the engine proletariat'.[1]

This book describes the Yugoslav Army's organisation, stressing the differences between pre-1948 and later reorganisations during the conflict. It describes attempts by the Yugoslavs to establish an indigenous defence industry during this period, with the intention of overcoming the problem of supplying its army. It also covers the development of the first Yugoslav tank, a series of piston-engined fighters, several types of vessels for the Navy and a series of small arms.

The *Cominform Crisis* is the book that precedes *The Trieste Crisis 1953*, which was published as the first title in the Helion Europe@ War series. However, these two titles are complementary. The author suggests they should be read as two volumes of a single story in the events of the early Cold War in southeast Europe. In many cases, both books are in fact, the 'Yugoslav view' of both crises. Similar works that cover the 'other' side of both historical episodes are still to be written by other historians. However, the reader of this volume should note that such a book even with the 'Yugoslav view' was impossible until 20 years ago, due to research restrictions within the Yugoslav archives. This work is based on the author's research that covered several archives and museums based in Belgrade, Serbia. It also includes some archival sources related to organisational issues that are still kept in the Ministry of Defence. Finally, the author used the photographs that were previously unpublished and kept in the Media Centre of the Serbian Ministry of Defence.

This is the first history of this conflict and of the Yugoslav Army in this period, written in the English language.

1

TITO'S PARTISAN ARMY GOES INTO PEACETIME

Demobilisations as the Prerequisite for Peace Development

The end of the Second World War in May 1945 found the Yugoslav Army (which was until 1 March 1945, named the People's Liberation Army of Yugoslavia, or simply: the Partisan movement) mostly at the north-western borders of Yugoslavia disarming the different Axis and local anti-communist forces. Peace brought a new challenge; establishing communist rule. The Yugoslav Army with Marshal Josip Broz Tito at its head, was the only organised tool of the Communist Party of Yugoslavia for establishing power in the country. In fact, the Army in many cases replaced nonexistent civil authorities. During the late spring of 1945, its units moved from the west of Yugoslavia, into the centre of the country creating peacetime garrisons. Besides occasional clashes with the groups of local anti-communist forces that remained in nearly all parts of Yugoslavia, the peace brought many other problems: taking care of the logistics and security of a force containing nearly 800,000 men (as the official Yugoslav Army sources claimed), rebuilding damaged infrastructure, adapting to local surroundings and manning the border outposts.

The first parliamentary elections, held on 11 November 1945, confirmed the communist victory and Tito as the new Yugoslav leader. The monarchy was abolished and multi-party democracy was changed into 'People's Democracy'. The Army took an important

role in securing the elections and mobilising all of its cadres to take part in voting for 'Tito and Party'. As the communists secured their power, the Yugoslav Army started the process of demobilisation.

During the summer of 1945, a 'first wave' of demobilisation was organised, mostly including those who were needed for immediate service in civilian life as defined by the First Law of Demobilisation (issued on 19 July 1945). Another law of demobilisation was issued on 26 October 1945 and covered the youngest (born in 1928 and later), oldest (born 1919 and earlier) and women soldiers.[1] Interestingly, it was not applied until 15 November 1945 – after the election in which the communists formally took power in Yugoslavia and in which the Army took part. British sources in Yugoslavia estimated the size of the Army to be around 600,000, falling to around half a million in the election period. They said that the Army had been told how to vote and possibly, even told to vote twice at different voting places, thus securing over one million votes for Tito and the Party.[2]

This large wave of demobilisation was significant and even the controlled *Narodna Armija* magazine could not hide it, quoting the declaration of the Karlovac garrison 'Your return to your homes, means that we have finally won, which the latest elections confirm'.[3] The 'second wave' of demobilisation was a slow process taking almost a month and a half until the very end of 1945. It was a

De-mining of the Srem Plain, where a front with Axis forces had been established November 1944 – April 1945. One of the rare occasions that Yugoslav Army troops wore the Adrian helmets. (Medija Centar Odbrana)

the Yugoslav Army, et cetera[7]), waves of demobilisation and regular waves of recruitment, Tito's Army finally began its peacetime development.

Communist Ideology: 'Army – Forger of New Men'

The Law of Active Service in the Yugoslav Army (July 1946), claimed in its first article that the army 'was created from the people of Yugoslavia during the People's liberation struggle … and it was (amongst other things) the active carrier of Brotherhood and Unity'.[8] The role of the Communist Party in the creation of the new Yugoslav Army was never hidden. On the contrary, it was constantly stressed. The Yugoslav Army was the 'Great deed of the KPJ

complicated process: civilian clothes, meals and train transport had to be provided for every demobilised soldier or officer.[4]

The 'third wave' of demobilisation came in the autumn of 1946, from an order by Marshal Tito issued on 22 September 1946, excluding the personnel that served in the Guards and Interior Army (Corps for Yugoslav People's Defence, known by abbreviation KNOJ). It was carried out until the end of November and was labelled as 'another step to life in peace' and 'repeated proof of the peacefulness of our state and denied all the slanders which were heard from different sides'. This demobilisation included the personnel born between 1920 and 1923 who had joined the Partisans up to the end of 1944.[5]

In contrast, during September 1946, the process of recruiting new conscripts began, including those who had not served full-time in the military or did not serve at all and who were born between 1920 and 1927. The recruitment and arrival of new soldiers into Yugoslav Army units in the last week of November 1946, marked the final step in the transformation of the Partisan Army into the regular peacetime Yugoslav Army.[6] Combined with the set of necessary laws (Law on The Military Obligations of Citizens, Law of Service in

revolutionary creation'[9]

Building the new man (the new soldier) was a process which included the promotion of values that characterised communist ideology. In his planning text 'Our army – the forge of new people' published in 1946, one of the key Yugoslav communists and one of Tito's closest collaborators, Milovan Djilas, pointed out that the basic idea of Tito's army was the 'struggle for the freedom of the people, for workers' rights, for brotherhood and the equality of nations'. Djilas promoted the army as a nursery of 'new fighters for building the country' and finally, 'There is no greater honour and happiness but to be a part of that army … where day-by-day a new – braver, more determined, more cultural and wiser – man is being created'.[10]

Parts of the socialist identity embedded in the army would now assist in creating socialism in the country. According to the army media, the former soldier returns to his home as a *completely new man,* conducting the struggle, by organising the *zadrugas,* taking part in voluntary working actions and supporting the local party's organisation activities. The departure into civilian life was considered a departure to 'new battlegrounds of socialism'.[11] One of the soldiers stated: 'I left home as a farmer with the little knowledge that I acquired in elementary school and that was all … and today

De-mining was also a long and painstaking process in the Adriatic, lasting until the late 1940s. Here, Yugoslav Navy sailors are seen catching one such mine in the sea. (Medija Centar Odbrana)

Recruits from different areas of Yugoslavia having their hair cut before they receive their military uniforms. (Medija Centar Odbrana)

Adjusting the uniform of new Air Force recruits. (Medija Centar Odbrana)

Dressed in new uniforms and with typical military suitcases or 'coffers', new recruits enter their barracks. The inscription below Marshal Tito's portrait and above the entrance says: 'You are joining the Army: school and forger of new men'. (Medija Centar Odbrana)

Medical examination of the youngest generation of the soldiers in Skoplje garrison. (Medija Centar Odbrana)

I depart from it [the army], completely a new man able to actively participate in every place where the battle for socialism is being led'.[12] It was the same in other People's Democracy armies. In the Bulgarian Army there was a slogan: 'From the barracks (*kazarma*) to the economic front', giving further explanation: 'Barracks are schools for youths, who came from all sides of our Motherland … And when they leave barracks and return again to the villages, fields and enterprises, they should be well educated for life, to have all interests and to be an active builder of socialism in our state'.[13]

Commanding Cadres: Partisans and 'Former' Officers

The core of Tito's Army command cadres were officers that rose among the Partisan movement. They were differentiated by their pre-war education or background, their duration of Communist Party membership, their combat experience in the war and their personal skills. Officers or NCOs of the Royal Yugoslav Army (Serbs and some Slovenians) were rare in the Partisan movement. They remained loyal to the King and mostly fought the Partisans in the Yugoslav Army in the Fatherland, remained in POW camps in the

Reich, or became members of different formations that sided with Axis occupiers.

By the beginning of 1945, a number of Royal Yugoslav Army officers had arrived from POW camps in parts of Europe that had been liberated. Out of 440,750 Yugoslav servicemen that were in POW camps, around 350,000 returned to Yugoslavia, while the rest choose not to return to the communist rulership. Nearly 2,000 of the returnees joined the Partisan/Yugoslav Army. Almost the same number as the officers who had been accepted between late 1943 and 1945 from the Axis Croatian Homeland Force. Statistics from the end of the war showed that there were some 700 officers that had served previously in German, Italian, Bulgarian, Hungarian and Albanian forces or armies and had now joined the ranks of the new Yugoslav Army.[14]

It is very important to note that key Partisan commanders had been volunteers in the Spanish Civil War (1936–1939). Most of them were junior officers of the Spanish Republican Army. One of the important facts for understanding why Tito managed to survive Stalin's pressure and the Cominform Crisis was the presence of large numbers of Spanish veterans who held key positions in the Partisan movement and the Yugoslav Army. With their own personal 'revolutionary experience' and without direct Soviet involvement in their communist 'education', they were much more loyal to Tito than to Soviet or Comintern superiors.

By mid-1948, the Yugoslav Army had 49,100 officers. Amongst them 8,500 were political officers or 'commissars', while a further

A typical classroom in one of the units of the Osijek garrison reveals the ideology of 'brotherhood and unity' that was one of the cornerstones of the Yugoslav Army in the Cold War era. (Medija Centar Odbrana)

In most of the barracks, walls were adorned with different ideological murals or scenes from the 'revolution', the Partisan 'struggle', or everyday life in the army. (Medija Centar Odbrana)

1,600 belonged to the military security service. The officers were 52 percent Serbs, 22 percent Croats, 11 percent Montenegrins, 8.4 percent Slovenians, four percent Macedonians and 2.6 percent of other 'nationalities'. By social background they were 44 percent peasants and 27.4 percent workers, prior to war. It was estimated that more than 50 percent had lower ranks than the duty to which they were assigned. Promotions became much more frequent in the later phases of the Cominform Crisis, which coincided with the establishment of various higher officers' and specialist schools. Generally, the largest problem in Tito's Army was a lack of proper civil and military education at almost all levels of command.[15]

One of the peculiar characteristics of Tito's Yugoslavia was that most of the members of the Central Committee of the Communist Party or the republican leadership, were promoted to general rank – at least 30 of them were generals. Many of them wore uniforms, despite being appointed to civilian and Party duties. 'Pure' military generals were assigned to the Ministry of People's Defence, the General Staff, the Ground Force armies, the Air Force, the Navy, KNOJ and UDBA HQs. The lowest ranking generals were those who commanded the elite proletarian or rifle divisions. Until the end of 1947, the highest military rank in the Yugoslav Army (except for Marshal Tito) was Lieutenant-General. On 22 December 1947, the first eight Colonel Generals (three-star generals) were promoted. Three of them being the members of the Central Committee and five at the highest positions in the Army.[16]

Other analyses of Tito's generals show several peculiarities. In the period 1945–1948, over 50 percent of generals were aged between 34 and 43 years of age, while 20 percent were around 30 years of age. Tito was older than his generals by between 15 and 25 years and this justified his nickname of 'Stari' (Old man) in the higher party and army echelons. The charisma associated with his age was also one of the explanations for how he managed to maintain his authority over most of his subordinates. The Montenegrins were most peculiar in this sense: their 'leaders' in the military and party were aged between 18 and 35 and made up 89 percent with just 11 percent older than 35.[17] In normal conditions, they would have been junior officers or senior NCOs. But most of them held senior officer rank, even general rank and commanded the largest army units or were their political commissars.

Examining the nationality of some 160 Yugoslav Army generals – not counting those who had general rank but were on civil or party duties – in the first decade after the Second World War, reveals that:[18]

- Around 30 percent were Serbs, born in Austro-Hungary (Bosnia, Herzegovina, Croatia, Krajina/former Military Border, Slavonia, Vojvodina, Dalmatia).

Yugoslav Infantry in the Victory day parade, Belgrade 1946. (Medija Centar Odbrana)

- A further 30 percent were from Montenegro (Serbs from Montenegro, since 1945 a separate Montenegrin nation), which meant that two third of Tito's generals were Serbs born out of Serbia proper.

No matter the strength of communist ideology, the officers of Tito's Army came from various backgrounds: Partisans, former Royal Yugoslav Army officers that had spent their wartime in POW camps and those who were members of different wartime formations. Here, at a military parade in Belgrade, 1948. (Medija Centar Odbrana)

- The remaining 30 or so percent consisted of Slovenes, Croats (12–13 percent each) and Serbs (7 percent), from Serbia itself. It is important to note that Serbs from Serbia were missing from the higher (general) military cadres of Tito's Army. In the case of Croatia, it is also obvious that Croats from Croatia proper were also missing. The majority were born in Dalmatia or Bosnia-Herzegovina. There were only a couple of Macedonians among the generals. A few remaining generals were of Czech, Russian or Jewish origin but all of them were born inside Yugoslavia's borders.[19] Such a national background of Tito's generals was regarded by prominent Croatian opposition politician Bogdan Radica as the 'vertical uprising of the south-Slav periphery' against 'static stand [general passivity] of Serbia and proper Croatia'.[20]

This national structure may suggest Serb dominance in the post-war Yugoslav Army but in fact, membership of the Communist Party and Partisan movement was crucial. Tito's generals did not perceive themselves as Serbs but in nearly all cases, as communists, internationalists and later as Yugoslavs. It is important to stress that over 10 percent of generals in this period were former officers of the Spanish Republican Army. Those were nearly all of the first-promoted generals who commanded the armies of the ground forces in the spring of 1945. They also included: Tito's deputy as Minister of Defence, the Chief of the General Staff, the head of the Communist Party organisation in the Army, the chiefs of the different branches such as intelligence, medical and armoured units and the head of the operative department of UDBA,

The official language of the Yugoslav Army was Serbo-Croatian. In the early post-war years, the written language was mostly in Cyrillic and much less in the Roman alphabet – usually the 'jekavica' version, as spoken in Montenegro, Bosnia and Herzegovina and Croatia. After the start of the 1950s, it was standardised and the military language was Serbo-Croat. The 'ekavian' version – as spoken in Serbia proper – and written in Roman ('latinica'), was the practice in the western part of Yugoslavia. It was a good symbiosis, representing the policy of 'Brotherhood and Unity' between Serbs and Croats (Bosniak Muslims were still not defined as a separate nation from those two). Slovenians, Macedonians and other minorities had to become accustomed to this practice. During this time, regional differences were not allowed. After 1945, most of the commands, titles and vocabulary used in the Army was inherited from Royal Yugoslav/Serbian Army. In the period between 1946 and 1951, the influence of Soviet and other terminology can be seen but this was later replaced with the earlier terms and practice.[21]

Peacetime Organisation of the Yugoslav Army

During 1945, even while the war was still in its concluding phases, the temporary government of Democratic Federative Yugoslavia formed a Ministry of Defence amongst

The Soviet T-34 main battle tank was the core tank in the Yugoslav Army until the beginning of the 1950s, with over 420 examples in use. This photo reveals behind the T-34 (serial 1016) a tank company with T-34s on the right and a self-propelled artillery company on the right, featuring Hetzers, an SU-76 and a Bren/Universal carrier on the left side. (Medija Centar Odbrana)

A number of Jagdpanzer 38 (t) Hetzer tank destroyers were captured by the Yugoslav Army in the late stages of the Second World War. Some of them were used by the newly created tank brigades and at least half a dozen by the Tank Military School as is this example with tactical number '3'. (Medija Centar Odbrana)

One of two Stuarts light tanks that were converted by the 1st Tank Brigade during operations in 1945 into anti-tank weapons by adding a German PAK 75mm anti-tank gun. This example is seen leading a column of AEC armoured cars during one of the military parades in Belgrade, 1946. (Medija Centar Odbrana)

the other civilian ministries. Leader of the Yugoslav Partisan Movement and Secretary General of the Yugoslav Communist Party, Josip Broz Tito, became Minister of Defence. Tito remained in the position of Minister of Defence until the state reforms of 1953. He also held the function of the Supreme Commander, being the President of the Republic from 1945 until his death in 1980. He was awarded the rank of marshal in late November 1943 by the 'Anti-Fascist Council of Yugoslav People's Liberation', a kind of provisional, communist-led government. The rank of marshal did not exist in previous Royal Yugoslav or the Serbian Army. The rank of marshal was a good choice: it corresponded with similar ranks among the Allies and Soviets alike, outmatching eventual competitors among the Royal Yugoslav Army – in the Fatherland or those with Allied forces. As 'supreme commander' he maintained undisputed authority over the Yugoslav Army until the end of his life.[22]

The Ministry of People's Defence as an institution was in fact, controlled by the Deputy Minister, General Ivan Gošnjak. In the beginning, this was a temporary solution but Gošnjak remained in power and even became the 'full' Minister of Defence in 1953. He served in that position until 1967. Through a system of ministerial deputies and assistants, the Ministry maintained control over the Ground Forces armies, Navy, Air Force, Interior Army/ KNOJ, military academies or schools, plus other HQs and specific units. Later, most of the operational command links were transferred to the General Staff. Different departments were established in the General Staff in March 1945 and later, in 1947, they received full control over the military structure of the Yugoslav Army. The Chief of General Staff during the later period acted as one of the Minister's assistants. Other assistants were responsible for personnel issues, political issues, the military security service and military industry.[23]

At the end of the Second World War, most of the Yugoslav Army HQs were in the northwest of Yugoslavia, in Slovenia. On 31 May 1945, Tito ordered a reorganisation of the Yugoslav Army ground forces into six armies. The Army HQs were established in Kragujevac (First), Zagreb (Second), Novi Sad (Third), Ljubljana (Fourth), Skopjle (Fifth) and Sarajevo (Sixth).[24] A short lived First Tank Army with only two half-sized divisions, was soon disbanded and its units were transferred to 'commands' made up of tank and motorised units.[25] Some other branches, such as artillery or anti-aircraft artillery soon had such 'commands' established as well.

An Interior Army called the Corps for Yugoslav People's Defence, or simply KNOJ, was established in the spring of 1944 and by the autumn of 1945 it had reached the strength of nine divisions. The KNOJ was responsible for border protection and interior security. KNOJ units, scattered all over the country, hunted the

A rare sight in the Yugoslav Army armoured inventory was this Canadian Ford Lynx armoured car. It was used as a command vehicle, seen here at a parade in Belgrade, 1946. (Medija Centar Odbrana)

Two Junkers JU-W-34 single-engined transports were used by the Transport Aviation Regiment, based at the Zemun/Belgrade airport. Later they were passed to Yugoslav Airlines-JAT who used them for miscellaneous duties including agricultural spraying, such in this example marked as YU-ACG. (Author's Collection)

remaining local anti-communist forces, acting upon the orders of the OZNA (and later the UDBA) security service.[26]

The new Yugoslav Air Force had a different inheritance in personnel and equipment to the Army: former Royal Yugoslav Air Force personnel that came from Yugoslav units within RAF, USAAF or POW camps, personnel that had served in the Croatian Air Force during the war and those who were Partisans and were trained in the Soviet Union. Its equipment was a true blend of aircraft from the RAF, the Soviet Air Force and the different Axis Air Forces that had operated in occupied Yugoslavia.[27] In the period between 1945 and 1948, it had grown to a size of five aviation divisions with four strike aviation regiments (equipped with Ilyushin Il-2), four fighter regiments (Yakovlev Yak 1/3/9/9P, Messerschmitt Bf.109G), three bomber regiments (Petlyakov Pe-2), one reconnaissance regiment (Supermarine Spitfire, Hawker Hurricane), one light bomber regiment (Polikarpov Po-2) and one transport regiment (Lisunov Li-2, Douglas C-47, Junkers Ju-52 and Ju-W-34, plus other types). There was a Military Air Academy with three 'school' regiments (Po-2, Yakovlev Ut-2, Ikarus Aero-2, de Havilland Tiger Moth, North American Harvard and others). All other ground units of the Air Force were subordinated to four air territorial commands,

which later styled divisions. Most of the combat units were located on five main bases: Zemun/Belgrade, Pleso/Zagreb and Sombor with concrete runways, plus Skopjle and Mostar with grass runways. School units were scattered at several airfields in south Banat.[28]

The Yugoslav Navy actually 'built itself' during the war, by the efforts of the Partisan forces on the Adriatic. It mostly operated various kinds of civilian vessels and boats termed 'armed ships' if they were larger, or 'patrol boats' if they were of a smaller size. Most of those vessels were, by the orders issued in mid-June 1945, returned to previous owners or to the civilian maritime department for use in civilian life. At the end of the war, a small number of German patrol boats, landing or auxiliary vessels were captured.[29]

After the decision that Royal Yugoslav Navy – which operated with Royal Navy in Mediterranean – should be disbanded and its vessels returned to Yugoslavia, Tito's Navy got an important influx of vessels to fill its fleet. These were a single corvette and a submarine, nine different motor gunboats, four minelayers, four customs patrol boats, three auxiliary ships and a single yacht. Together with other captured vessels the fleet – established on 18 July 1945 – had the following units as of 1 September 1945: Motor Gunboat Squadron, Torpedo Boat Squadron, Minelayer Flotilla and Landing

Belonging to the Royal Yugoslav Navy, which operated them from Malta (1943–1945), were seven PT-201 Motor Gunboats (known in Yugoslav service simply as 'Higgins'). They are seen here in Split harbour after their arrival in Yugoslavia in September 1945. They were numbered from 1 to 7, later changed to 101 to 107, being rearmed with 450mm torpedoes. In the back is *Kajmakčalan* Motor Gunboat, numbered 6. (Medija Centar Odbrana)

Flotilla. They operated a total of 57 different vessels, among them 30 combat and 27 auxiliary ones.[30] The other parts of the Yugoslav Navy included: three naval district HQs that covered the Adriatic Coast and which controlled other naval units such as naval infantry, coastal artillery, technical workshops, storages and hospitals. A variety of Naval Schools were created, from the Naval Academy to different NCO technical schools. Finally, there was the River Flotilla which operated on the Sava and Danube Rivers.[31]

The Yugoslav military high command decided that the most applicable model for the post-war Yugoslav Army organisation, was the Soviet one. Soon after the war was over, the Partisan divisions were reorganised upon the Soviet pattern: three rifle brigades, an artillery brigade and other minor units.[32] Tank units were organised into tank divisions comprised of two brigades, each of two tank battalions. Lower units also adopted the three-unit structure. With the process of demobilisation, this adoption of the Soviet organisation led to a downsizing of the Yugoslav Army and slow adaption to peacetime service. Following the Soviet pattern, which Yugoslavs introduced on 15 March 1946, they were given covert titles for their units: real names were hidden with 'military post', five-digit numbers.[33] The title of the unit was declared a military secret. In the military and other press reports, the names of the units were hidden by using 'unit of commander so and so' or in the beginning, as 'N unit' – this later disappeared when they followed the Soviet pattern.

After the arrival of the second conscript contingent in November 1946, the Guards Division was formed with three brigades, plus cavalry, artillery and other miscellaneous units. Its main task was protecting Marshal Tito at his main residence in Belgrade and other residences in different parts of Yugoslavia.[34]

In March 1947, a reorganisation was ordered, concerning mostly the Ministry of Defence and General Staff departments, reducing the number of rifle and KNOJ divisions and also the adoption of military territorial departments to the organisation of the civilian communities. Now, Yugoslav ground forces had 27 rifle divisions and five newly formed independent rifle brigades. The KNOJ was reduced to four divisions for interior purposes and six to seven border regiments.[35]

It is worth noting that the Yugoslav Army was constantly reducing its manpower in this first post-war period. On 31 December 1946, it had 575,653 men (31,953 officers, 38,370 NCOs, 505,330 soldiers). On 31 December 1947, the Yugoslav Army had 366,900 'formation places' while 293,782 were present ('on the face').[36] The period between 1945 and 1947 saw the largest reductions. By the beginning of 1948, the Yugoslav Army had somehow stabilised having still a huge figure of over 300,000 men.

The need for the education of new officers and the additional training for the numerous Partisan cadres without proper or any, military schooling was paramount. Immediately after the war, during the summer and autumn of 1945, many academies and schools were formed. The General Staff issued an order on 31 July 1945 for the organisation of schools and academies in the Yugoslav Army. Upon this order, a number of schools and academies had to start working by 20 September 1945. They were named in the Soviet style *uchilishte* – later during the Cominform Crisis these were mostly changed to *akademija* or academy. There were establishments for infantry, artillery, tanks, engineers, signals and aviation. Several other smaller schools were created for the education of the officers of different logistical and technical branches and the further education of Partisan officers.[37] The Yugoslav Army adopted the Soviet concept of military schools mostly upon the influence of Soviet Advisors and the influence of those Yugoslav cadres who arrived from Soviet academies and schools during 1945. As General Klisanic wrote in late 1945, 'The organisation of military schools and academies

Yugoslav marine infantry, seen here in September 1946, kept the influence of their appearance from British Royal Marine Commandos that operated in Adriatic during 1944–1945. (Medija Centar Odbrana)

used by the Red Army, provides us with a high ideal and safe route forward'.[38]

The Infantry Academy was established in Belgrade and in late 1947, transferred to Kragujevac. The Armoured Academy was also established in Belgrade in 1945 but the next year moved to Bela Crkva in Banat where the possibilities for training were much better.[39] The Artillery Academy, Artillery Technical Academy, Artillery Officers School and Air Defence Officers School started work in Zagreb barracks in the late autumn of 1945. The Engineers Officer School in Karlovac and the Communication Officers School and Academy in Belgrade, were formed in the same period.[40]

The Air Academy started working in September 1945 by transforming the 1st Pilot School previously established with RAF-supplied aircraft in Zadar. This school was then transferred to Pančevo and several other minor airfields in south Banat, where the training of the first pilot class started. Several other air technical schools were reorganised in 1947 into the Air Technical Academy for training the technicians, signals and other branches needed for the Air Force, mostly based in Kraljevo.[41] The Military Naval Academy was formed officially on 2 February 1947, after the premises and resources of the Royal Naval Academy in Dubrovnik were reconstructed during the autumn of 1946. During the following autumn, the Academy was moved to Divulje, near Split. In this previous home of the Austro-Hungarian and Royal Yugoslav Navy, a Military Naval-Technical Academy was also formed in December 1947.[42]

In 1947, the education of reserve officers started within the existing academies and schools. Training included one year of schooling and another year in the units, at the lowest level of command.[43] The best cadets in every class in each of the academies or schools were called 'Tito's cadets' and were especially rewarded.

Armament and Equipment

The Partisan Army grew from the communist-led resistance movement and at the end of the Second World War turned into a large army, possibly having as many as 800,000 troops. Partisan units varied in size, equipment and personnel. Part of the divisions which were in the east of Yugoslavia were rearmed from late 1944 and into 1945, with Soviet equipment. The other divisions which were in Dalmatia and alongside the Adriatic, were equipped with British or American equipment. Most of the others were equipped with captured equipment and weaponry from different Axis forces. At the end of the war, in parts of Slovenia, huge quantities of Axis heavy equipment were captured enabling Tito's Army to organise heavy artillery, anti-aircraft artillery, engineer, communications, technical and other units.

The process of gathering the war booty that was captured or abandoned in Slovenia lasted throughout the late spring and summer of 1945. During this period the Main War Trophy Base, with its HQ in Zagreb, was tasked to recover and then gather equipment before sending it on to the units.[44] The repair of such equipment was a 'heavy burden'. First Tank Army HQ reported: 'We do not have enough workshops or workers' for the task. It was judged that the best solution, was to rearm 'all of our units … with Russian equipment'.[45]

After the six armies of the ground forces were formed at the end of May 1945, a process of standardisation of equipment started at the level of rifle divisions (either Soviet or German equipment) creating the artillery, engineer, anti-tank, anti-aircraft and other sub-units within the six armies. Miscellaneous units such as communication, medical and chemical were still not formed and were created as the needed equipment was assembled from stocks or delivered from the Soviet Union. Part of the artillery, anti-tank or anti-aircraft artillery

A single Soviet ISU-152 self-propelled howitzer, stuck in the mud in the autumn of 1944, was left to the Yugoslavs after the 2nd Ukrainian Front of the Soviet Army continued its dash into Hungary during the spring of 1945. It remained in use with the Yugoslav Tank Military School until the beginning of the 1950s. (Medija Centar Odbrana)

Numbers of different German artillery pieces were captured by the Partisans/Yugoslav Army in the late stages of the war. Here, a howitzer battery of the 17th Division at Radovljica are equipped with Le FH-18 105mm howitzers during training. (Medija Centar Odbrana)

produced in the different countries and previously used by the different forces were also used in the units.[47] Moreover, after late August 1945, Yugoslavia received a large quantity of lorries, other transport and specialised vehicles from the surplus stocks of the US, Canadian and British armies in Europe through the UNRRA programme.[48]

A kind of broader standardisation within the infantry divisions was carried out during 1946, creating Soviet and German equipped divisions. British, American, Italian and other equipment was concentrated in smaller units, the KNOJ, Air Force or Navy. Orders for standardisation were issued by the General Staff on 19 March 1948 (on the eve of the Cominform Crisis), which was then applied to standardise the armaments, heavy weaponry and other equipment within the armies, or different branches/services.[49] Despite these efforts, a wide variety of weapons and equipment remained one of the characteristics of the Yugoslav Army until American-supplied armaments and equipment entered the inventory from 1951.

Besides the general expectation that Soviet armaments and equipment would be delivered in vast quantities and become sufficient to standardise the Yugoslav Army inventory, it was soon discovered that this was not the case. Prior to the Cominform Crisis, initial steps in rebuilding the Yugoslavian weapons industry were made.

and engineer brigades were formed as part of the Reserve of the Supreme Command (RVK). They were later (in 1950) subordinated to the HQs of the armies or military districts where they were garrisoned.[46]

Looking at infantry weapons, there were numerous types of side-arms, rifles, submachine guns, machine guns and mortars of different production: German, Italian, Soviet, Yugoslav, British, American, French and Dutch. There were examples of almost all existing contemporary calibres: German 7.65mm, 7.9mm and 9mm, Italian 6.5mm and 8mm, Soviet 7.62mm, 12.7mm and 14.5mm, Yugoslav 7.9mm, British or American .303, .45, .5 and many others. It was a similar case with mortars which ranged from 50 to 120mm and artillery or anti-aircraft artillery. Many different types of vehicles

During March 1945, a team from the Ministry of People's Defence inspected what remained of Yugoslav military industrial capacity following the retreat of the German forces. The team's report was more a list of what had been destroyed, rather than what was capable of any kind of production.[50] After the war, the government issued an order on 20 June 1945 that 11 factories and plants that had previously been used for military production, should be transferred to the state ownership.[51]

During the inter-war period, the Yugoslav aviation industry had established several factories, mostly around Belgrade. What remained in 1945 – usable tools and other resources – were gathered in the Ikarus factory at Zemun/Belgrade airport.[52]

On 23 February 1946, the Yugoslav Air Force announced competitions for projects covering several aircraft types: a two-seat basic trainer, an advanced training two-seater, a two-engined training or transport aircraft and a light trainer aircraft. These were the continuation of the construction work that had started in 1940 but had been halted by the war. Prior to the Cominform Crisis, a batch of Ikarus Aero-2 basic trainers was built, based on a prototype which had been made in 1940. Prototypes of the other models were produced and/or built in smaller or larger series during the Cominform Crisis. Expecting assistance from the Soviet or other People's Democracy aviation industries, it was estimated that in the five years to 1951, a total of 860 aircraft could be built. After the disagreement with the Soviets started during March 1948, this ambitious target was reduced.[53]

The Yugoslav Army captured numerous German Sd. Kfz 250 and 251 half-tracks. They were used as command or anti-tank vehicles by the armoured units and interior KNOJ forces. Here, a Sd. Kfz Pak-Wagen, named 'Tito' leads a column of various Sd. Kfzs at the Sumadija manoeuvres, September 1949. (Medija Centar Odbrana)

Similar high targets were set by the Navy. It is interesting that the Yugoslav Navy commanders made ambitious plans for shipbuilding, even on 29 April 1945 when the war was still unfinished. The plan included the construction of nearly 50 different warships.[54] The extensive programme was outlined at the meeting of the Central Committee *Polit bureau* held on 24 December 1946.[55] A five-year plan of shipbuilding and development of the Navy was outlined in October 1947

Parked at Central Tank Workshop in the town of Mladenovac in 1946 are German K-2670 Steyr railroad armoured cars. Contrary to German practice, who combined them to create this powerful armoured train, the Yugoslavs used them as separate vehicles attached to KNOJ until the beginning of the 1950s. Beyond is a motley line-up of different damaged or defective Italian and French tanks used by different Axis forces in occupied Yugoslavia during the Second World War. (Author's Collection)

and signed in March 1948. But as the Cominform Crisis started, it had to be changed during the next year.[56]

During 1947, production of rifle mortar and 85mm artillery ammunition and hand grenades began. Production started with generally high expectations from Yugoslav Army commanders, which were still difficult to fulfil.[57] The Ministry of People's Defence sent representatives to Czechoslovakia and Poland to investigate obtaining tools or even purchasing whole factories. According to General Pavle Jakšić, contracts for two armament factories were signed.[58]

The sudden outbreak of the Cominform Crisis changed nearly all those unreal expectations and the plans for the reestablishment of Yugoslavia's military industry. Despite the unreal expectations, most of Yugoslavia's Cold War military industry would be built during this crisis. In one of his speeches in 1950, Tito commented on this

pre-crisis neglect of the indigenous military industry by saying: 'We were misled at that time, by the illusion that we could rely on the Soviet Union. That we did not need our own factories for production of different types of armament for our Army. We believed their word that they would provide us with brotherly help, that they would give us the required weapons'.[59]

Security and Intelligence Services

All of Yugoslavia's Cold War security services emerged from a single service: the Department for the Protection of the People (locally well-known upon the abbreviation: OZNA, *Odeljenje za zaštitu naroda*). The OZNA was formed on 13 May 1944, in the Bosnian city of Drvar. At that time, in the city there was the HQ of the Partisan Main Staff with Marshal Tito and the Allied and Soviet liaison missions. On 15 August 1944, a Corps for People's Defence (KNOJ)

Officers of the Army Counterintelligence Service known by its abbreviation KOS. (N. Nikolić)

According to the initial organisation, KOS had the following organisation: departments at the level of Ministry of People's Defence and the HQs of armies, Air Force, Navy and KNOJ; sections at the level of the divisions and similar level HQs; and sub-sections at the brigades, regiments, military schools and military enterprises. The lower-level units were assigned KOS officers or NCOs. At the beginning of 1948, all KOS organisational elements received the number XII (12) as their prefix. This number remained as a kind of synonym for the whole service.[65] By the beginning of 1948, KOS had 1,618 personnel, growing in the first year of the Cominform Crisis to around 1,900 men.[66]

was formed. It was the interior military force, whose members carried out tasks upon the orders of the OZNA representatives in the regions. The roles of OZNA and KNOJ were to purge so-called 'People's Enemies' and the establishing of the interior affairs of all Yugoslavian republics, following their liberation.[60]

This service was headed by Aleksandar Ranković, one of Tito's closest allies. He was a member of the Partisan Main HQ and the highest council of the Yugoslav Communist Party, the Central Committee. He had previously been tasked with organisational and personnel issues.[61]

It is important to note that Tito and his close collaborators relied heavily on their experiences of pre-war illegal communist practices and combating their opponents in the civil war that raged in occupied Yugoslavia, rather than the simple adoption of Soviet models. But OZNA improved its capabilities with training from similar Soviet services and the introduction of their operational and ideological methods. As well as around 3,000 army personnel who were trained in Soviet military academies and military schools in the period between 1944 and 1948, a total of 29 members from the OZNA departments in each republic were sent to the NKVD academy in Moscow. Upon finishing the six-month training programme, they were returned to their departments where they organised further training courses for the other members of the service.[62]

After the first constitutional changes in spring 1946, the OZNA split into two services: the Department for the State Security (known as UDBA, *Uprava državne bezbednosti*) and the Counterintelligence Service within the Yugoslav Army (KOS, *Kontraobaveštajna služba*). Head of the KOS was Colonel Jefto Šašić, who had been the chief of the III Department of the OZNA from its foundation in 1944.[63] Later promoted to rank of general, Šašić remained in the power until 1964, becoming almost synonymous with the KOS and military security affairs as far as the wider Yugoslav public were concerned. Formally, the head of the KOS was subordinated to the Assistant Minister for the People's Defence that was tasked with ideological affairs and the work of the Communist Party organisation inside the Yugoslav Army.[64]

It is interesting to note, that the OZNA and its later successor UDBA, was headed by the Yugoslav Ministry of Interior (Ranković) and the republic's Ministries of Interior. Although it was the service with an interior role, it was also subordinated to the Ministry of Defence. The UDBA budget was included in the defence budget, its members had military ranks and wore army uniforms. The system of training was through similar courses to the army. The UDBA even used the so-called, military post number system to hide the real titles of some subordinated units and establishments. It was quite an unusual dualism.

Unlike the Counterintelligence Service, which was in fact the security service for operating inside army units, Yugoslav Army Intelligence was part of the General Staff. During the later decades, it would be known as the VOS (*Vojno-obaveštajna služba* – Military Intelligence Service), which did not sound so dramatic as *Kontraobaveštajna služba*. Initially just referred to as II Section, from March 1947, it was enlarged into II Intelligence Department with the addition of a radio-surveillance section. The service had sections in the largest HQs (Ground Force Armies, Air Force, Navy) and smaller detachments or intelligence officers in the lower-level units, divisions, brigades and regiments.[67]

Most of the reports and other preserved documents from 1946–1949 suggest that intelligence work in the early post-war years was oriented against the Allied forces around Trieste, their forces in Italy, Austria and Greece, or the local Italian or Greek Army. This coincided with Yugoslav expectations and plans that the next war would be centred around Trieste or at the Italian border and as a secondary front, against Greece. The other neighbouring armies that belonged to the People's Democracy movement (Hungary, Rumania, Bulgaria and Albania) were not the subject of intelligence tasking. Moreover, intelligence was not regarded by the Yugoslav Army high command (all of them former Partisans) as important as counterintelligence. In 1945 and 1946, two groups of Yugoslav Army officers (JA, Jugoslovenska armija) finished seven and a half month's intelligence courses in the Soviet Army. Initial intelligence training in Yugoslavia started in late 1947 but a much greater emphasis was placed on intelligence training in the years after the outbreak of the

Cominform Crisis. The main problem was the lack of intelligence knowledge and fluency in foreign languages. [68]

The other means of gathering intelligence information was the work of Yugoslav military missions or military representatives (attaches) accredited in several neighbouring or allied countries, starting with the first military representative in August 1945 in France, and expanding to representatives in 14 countries by 1949. In the case of Yugoslav military diplomats during this time, a lack of language skills, proper training and tasking added to firm communist standpoints, meant that the VOS credited its work with weak or no results. [69] The Cominform Crisis would show many problems with the gathering of intelligence. The reforms and improvements needed in intelligence practice was noted from 1949 and later. However, Yugoslav military intelligence always lagged behind the more ideologically important counterintelligence and security services.

2
THE SOVIETISATION OF THE YUGOSLAV ARMY

At end of the Second World War the Yugoslav Army was flushed with victory. This was bolstered by the feeling of power produced by the notion that the great victorious force – the Red Army – were their closest ally and the largest supporter of the former Partisans who now grew into the regular army of new Yugoslavia. In such circumstances, it was expected that the pattern for the peacetime reconstruction of the Yugoslav Army would be the Soviet Red Army, without any specific decision or decree. Ideological influence, technical support and training Yugoslavs in the Soviet academies was followed by the arrival of Soviet Advisors who were tasked to give comradely assistance to a smaller ideological brother. Following disputes on the Italian border with British and American troops in May 1945, a decision was made that in any future war, the Yugoslav Army could only fight shoulder-to-shoulder with the Soviets against the Western capitalists. [1]

In the period between late 1945 and late 1948, the Soviet Union was perceived as the 'guarantee of our freedom, independence and progress', the 'main and only honest ally of the Partisan movement in Yugoslavia', the 'pattern for state of happiness and welfare' and the 'keeper of war and the saviour of mankind from fascism and barbarity'.[2] Prior to the establishment of the Warsaw Pact in 1955, the Yugoslav, Bulgarian, Czechoslovak and Polish militaries found a broader international community in 'Slavic Unity' (in Bulgarian: 'slaviansko edinstvo') and a brotherhood with the armies 'of other Slavic states' (in Bulgarian: 'na drugite slavianski strani'). The Soviet Union and its army was, of course, at the forefront.[3]

In the immediate post-war years, in many areas of society, a new species of human being, a 'Homo Sovieticus' was celebrated and promoted as the example that all should emulate. Military language

Marshal Tito is seen here accompanying Yugoslav Air Force Colonel France Pirc and an unknown Soviet senior officer at Zemun/Belgrade airport on 16 September 1945. The ceremony was to welcome the 1st Yugoslav (later the 254th and 83rd) Fighter Regiment from the Soviet Union. This unit was formed from Yugoslav personnel trained in Krasonodar in southern Russia. They were equipped with Yak-3 fighters and returned to Yugoslavia in mid-September. (Medija Centar Odbrana)

During 1946 Soviet engineer units repaired the bridge over the River Danube which was the sole connection between the capital of Belgrade and wider area of Banat. The first photo has three Soviet soldiers overlooking the work on the bridge and the second shows the monument built near the bridge to mark those who had been proclaimed as the best workers or had distinguished themselves in some other way. (Medija Centar Odbrana)

During 1946, a batch of 52 Soviet SU-76 self-propelled guns re-equipped the artillery elements of the existing two armoured divisions. These examples participated in a Belgrade military parade held in 1947. The sign of the Yugoslav armoured units, a silhouette of the T-34 in a yellow or white disc, can be seen on the side of the turrets. (Medija Centar Odbrana)

Germans and to expand their fighting potential. There were two main agreements after the Second World War: the first on June 1946 and the second a year later in June 1947. The first agreement of 1946 was signed as a loan to Yugoslavia. According to this agreement a huge quantity of 308 T-34 main battle tanks (coupled with spare 76mm tank guns) and 52 SU-76 self-propelled guns, were passed to Yugoslavs. This purchase enabled Yugoslavs to rearm their two armoured divisions and later, to establish a new one in 1950.

Yugoslav artillery was also incorporated in these purchases. It had received large quantities of different calibre guns and howitzers such as: 235 anti-tank guns calibre 45mm, over 820 regimental or anti-tank guns calibre 76mm, over 310 gun/howitzer calibre 122mm, 20 gun/howitzers calibre 152mm and almost 700 mortars of two main calibres, 82mm and 120mm. These purchases were supported with the necessary ammunition, equipment and tools which completely equipped the Yugoslav Army first line artillery units.[6]

According to the agreements of 1946, Yugoslav anti-aircraft artillery units received almost 300 AA guns calibre 37mm. They were used for establishing the AA units of the ground forces as well as for the establishment of light territorial AA defence. The second agreement of 1947 brought more artillery weapons and equipment including: 220 heavier 85mm AA guns, 60 more 37mm AA guns, plus quantities of artillery calculators, reflectors and other equipment. Finally, nine surveillance P-2M radars and one ship-born GJUIS-1M radar were added to this inventory.[7]

Other delivered equipment included over 71,000 rifles, 55,000 submachine guns, over 600 anti-tank rifles, 100 AA machine guns, over 3,000 radio sets, 1,000 various engineer boats, 1,000 tons of powder, hundreds of millions rounds of ammunition, chemical warfare equipment and much more.[8]

also altered. Whole lists of typical Soviet military phrases and terminology were introduced.

Deliveries of Soviet Weaponry 1944–1948

One of the main aspects of Yugoslav-Soviet military relations was Soviet technical support to the Yugoslav Army. During 1944, Moscow supplied the Yugoslav Partisan forces with a vast number of Soviet made weapons that helped it grow into a full scale army. Tito signed an agreement in Moscow in September 1944 whereby the Soviets provided complete weaponry for the rearming of 12 Partisan divisions.[4] They also passed to the Yugoslavs, two complete aviation divisions, organised in the Soviet Union an infantry and a tank brigade, plus two more aviation regiments and provided deliveries of large amounts of other equipment and armaments.[5]

In the post-war period, the Soviets greatly assisted in the modernisation of the Yugoslav Army with purchases of equipment which had started during the final stages of war. Several agreements between the Soviet and Yugoslav military authorities were ratified in the following two years. This enabled the Yugoslavs to continue the process of replacing different equipment captured from the

Various types of Soviet artillery pieces delivered to Yugoslav Army: ML-20 or M-1937 152mm gun-howitzer. A total of 20 were obtained but a few examples were captured from the Germans in 1944/45. Here, an example belonging to the Artillery School in Zagreb, 1948.

ZIS-3 or M-1942 76mm divisional gun – in Yugoslavia used mostly later as anti-tank gun. Here, as part of the 62nd Infantry Division, Pančevo 1950.

KS-12 or M-1939 85mm anti/aircraft gun, belonging to the AA Artillery Regiment in Zemun, 1952. (Medija Centar Odbrana)

Ilyushin Il-2 Shturmoviks were delivered in several batches during 1945 and became the backbone of the Yugoslav strike aviation serving in four strike regiments and a training unit. (Milan Micevski Collection)

A batch of 11 Lisunov Li-2 transports were delivered to Yugoslavia in the summer of 1945. They were incorporated into the 1st Transport Aviation Regiment, based in Zemun/Belgrade airport. In 1946, some of them were used in the first steps of establishing civilian air transport, organised by the YAF HQs Civil Aviation Department. The civil registrations in YU-BAA to BAF range were provisional and later removed. (Medija Centar Odbrana)

Production of the Yugoslav Ikarus Aero-2 trainer created a dispute between the representatives of the two Air Forces. The Yugoslavs had their own pre-war experiences and projects and wanted to continue with them. On the other side, the Soviets claimed that the existing UT-2 and Po-2 training types were sufficient for the Yugoslav Air Force. (VOC)

of August 1945, 11 Lisunov Li-2 and six Šćerbakov Šće 2 transports were passed to the Yugoslavs, which helped them to establish their Transport Aviation Regiment. Yugoslav aviation personnel in Sombor, waiting for a Soviet bomber division to be passed to them in late August 1945, were surprised when a batch of 64 Petlyakov Pe-2s arrived being flown by women. After the end of the war, the Soviets were in the process of disbanding all surplus units. One such women 'manned' division, was passed to Yugoslavia to establish its bomber force. In September and October of the same year, over 100 light Polikarpov Po-2s and Yakovlev UT-2Ms were delivered to Yugoslavia for the formation of three school/ training regiments of its newly established *Vazduhoplovno vojno učilište* – the Air Force Academy.[10] The Yugoslav Air Force, was completely technically dependent on Soviet deliveries. Following large purchases in 1945, the process continued in the following years when further deliveries of assault IL-2s with metal fuselages and training UT-2s (1947). Even 40 examples of the Soviet's most modern fighter, the Yakovlev Yak-9P, were delivered prior to the start of the Cominform Crisis in 1948.

The Yugoslav Navy listed its requirements to Soviet military negotiators but did not receive most of the ordered equipment and vessels, especially torpedo boats which were the subject of later Yugoslav complaints.

Yugoslavs complained constantly that there were problems with deliveries of spare parts, equipment, ammunition and fuel. The Soviets were not reliable suppliers, most likely because of other priorities elsewhere

The Yugoslav Air Force especially benefited from Soviet cooperation. In June 1945, one strike aviation regiment with 40 Il-2 Shturmoviks, arrived in Yugoslavia after training and equipping in the USSR. In September 1945, another fighter regiment with 35 Yak-3s reached Zemun/Belgrade airport.[9]. At the very beginning and later due to the slow disintegration of the friendship with the Yugoslavs. Sometimes the Soviets delivered incorrect or useless supplies. After the break with the Soviets, the Yugoslavs used to claim that despite the initial, very rapid and large scale deliveries, Soviet-supplied equipment had already been heavily used and only a small percentage of it passed general overhauls. To add to this, 50 percent of delivered tanks were without an electrical mechanism for turning the turret and only 75 percent of the accumulators were serviceable. Between the two agreements (1946 and 1947) and not included in those agreements, on 15 April 1947, there were deliveries of a further 35 SU-76 self-propelled guns, coupled with large batches of spare parts, engines, ammunition, equipment, tractors, special vehicles, tank transporters, trailers and van-workshops, all of which strengthened the Yugoslav armoured units.[11]

Finally, one of the disputes that occurred during this period of 'comradely friendship' was a Yugoslav project for an indigenous, light primary-training aeroplane announced in 1946. Soviet technical representatives and advisors

Two of the Soviet-produced river gunboats, type 1124 and 1125 served in the River Flotilla based in Sabac on the Sava River. Of note are the T-34/76mm turrets on both gunboats. (Medija Centar Odbrana)

in Yugoslavia were angry that the Yugoslavs had complaints about the airworthiness of Soviet Po-2 and UT-2 trainers. The Yugoslavs wanted to replace these types with a new one, such as the Ikarus Aero-2, which would be more suited to the Yugoslav basic training process.[12]

Soviet Advisors in the Yugoslav Army

The presence of Soviet Advisors made a significant impact on the development of the Yugoslav Army. By the late stages of the war, Soviet Advisors had already entered the Partisan/Yugoslav Army units in large numbers. At least 117 of them were deployed at the end of 1944.[13]

After the war, Soviet Advisors started to enter all Yugoslav Army command levels from Army HQs to independent regiments. Their presence was specially emphasised in the Yugoslav military schools. On 31 December 1945, there were a total of 115 Soviet Advisors in the Yugoslav Army.[14] The numbers did fluctuate though, so it is difficult to estimate the exact number of Soviet officers in Yugoslavia

up to the Cominform Crisis. An analysis by the KOS dated 1950, counted 196 advisors, among them 31 definitely and seven probably, belonged to NKVD. The ten-year report of the KOS dated 1954, counted 'over 350'.[15]

General Kiselyev was chief of the Soviet military mission in Yugoslavia in 1945 and 1946 and his assistant was General Lotocky. In the period 1947–1948, the chief of the mission was General Obarskov. The Soviet military attaché in Belgrade was General Sidorovich during the whole period between 1945 and 1948.[16]

Soviet Advisors were most influential in Yugoslav military education and with the Air Force. The Yugoslav Army education system for its officers and NCOs started to be deeply influenced by process of 'Sovietisation'. Initially, there were no doubts about the value of Soviet experience and there was no evaluation of its suitability for training the Yugoslav Army. All materials were automatically translated without any corrections and passed directly

Soviet military advisors seen at one air show in Zemun/Belgrade airport during 1946, in joyful mood. (Medija Centar Odbrana)

Soviet military advisors to the Yugoslav Navy, seen here arriving at a ceremony at Split, September 1946. (Medija Centar Odbrana)

Some parts of the training of Yugoslav cavalry units were clearly influenced by the Soviet style, such as this standing on the saddle. (Medija Centar Odbrana)

As a vivid part of Sovietisation, the Yugoslav Army introduced the Soviet/Russian style of marching with an outstretched knee and replaced the traditional Yugoslav/Serbian marching pace, which is shortened by stretching the step in the knee. Here shows how this type of marching pace was trained (3rd Division Novi Sad, 1950, left) and adopted (45th Division, Sombor 1948, right). This style of marching was abandoned in 1952. (Medija Centar Odbrana)

The Soviet style collars of these cadets belonging to the Air Defence Artillery Academy clearly show the influence of Soviet patterns. (Medija Centar Odbrana)

to the schools. Large numbers of technical manuals for tanks, artillery and aircraft were distributed to the units. Combat-usage regulations, from the level of the single infantryman up to brigades, were also implemented. Many working hours were spent translating large numbers of Soviet military publications.[17]

For example, by the beginning of July 1945, Soviet military advisors and instructors were sent to the Yugoslav Military Academy. Later, Yugoslav remarks about them reported that they were young officers, promoted quickly to higher ranks following their reengagement after the war. Thus, they could not transfer serious knowledge to the Yugoslav cadets. They insisted that the

Soviet experience be paramount, introduced drill similar to patterns of the Soviet *Voenoe uchlishta* (military schools) and ignored previous Yugoslav Partisan and traditional Serbian/Yugoslav military experience. Yugoslavs thought their presence was useless.[18] The Infantry Officers School in Sarajevo had between eight and 10 Soviet Army instructors, ranked from colonels to majors. They were later accused, during the Cominform Crisis, of ignoring original experiences and being 'guilty' of implementing the strict drill that was introduced in this prestigious infantry school.[19]

In another example, the Soviet infantry tactics were introduced in the schools, even though they were useless in the Yugoslav situation. This produced several disputes between Yugoslav teachers and Soviet Advisors. The Russian language and the history of the Soviet

Communist Party were also introduced as mandatory courses for cadets. Soviet influence was evident in the introduction of Pedagogy and Psychology as courses in the Military Academy. However, all of the above-mentioned issues disappeared after 1948.

An additional source of influence came after 1947 when the first Yugoslavs returned after graduating as instructors from academies in the Soviet Union. They were junior officers and eager to show what they had learned in Soviet schools, becoming even stricter than the Soviet Advisors and were also the subject of complaints. For example, 18 of them sent to the Infantry Officers School were later criticised for insisting upon the harsh typical Soviet drill.[20]

From the beginning of the presence of Soviet military advisors in the Yugoslav Army, minor complaints and misunderstandings were present. As early as 1946, Tito had informed the Soviet government that the number of Soviet military specialists in Yugoslavia had to be reduced for financial reasons but Stalin bided his time.[21] For Yugoslav Foreign Minister Edvard Kardelj, it was a real shock when Stalin raised this question during their meeting on 19 April

The kind of servile Yugoslav relations with the Soviets can be seen in this photo, where a Yugoslav Air Force officer greets a Soviet dignitary. (Author's Collection)

1947. Kardelj replied that all misunderstandings, if they existed, should be settled on a comradely basis on both sides. Stalin's answer was sharp and without hesitation: 'Advisors are there to be listened to and not just to sit near you!' Kardelj tried to calm the situation, saying there was much truth in Stalin's words but continued that Yugoslavia had its own military knowledge and there should much better cooperation with the Soviet Advisors. The meeting concluded that there was no doubt about Soviet Advisors' efficiency.[22]

Yugoslav Personnel in Soviet Military Schools and Centres

In the later part of the Second World War, one of the most important parts of the cooperation between the Soviets and the Yugoslav Partisans was the training and education of Partisans in the Soviet Red Army military schools and academies. Late 1944 and the spring of 1945, saw tremendous numbers of Partisans sent to the Soviet Union for training. Military education in the Soviet academies attempted to create the most reliable component of Tito's officer corps, which was clearly supposed to fill the most important positions in the post-war armed forces.[23]

Air force personnel were the most needed for the young

Yugoslav pilots dressed in Soviet cadet uniforms, some of them wearing various wartime medals, pay close attention to their Soviet instructor, Koremovskaja, USSR. (L. Žanović Family)

Yugoslav fighter-pilot cadets during the 'flying day' with a Soviet instructor in the middle and a Yak fighter behind, Koremovskaja, USSR. (N. Milikić, L Žanović Families)

Typical Soviet memorabilia given to the members of a course prior to returning to Yugoslavia: 'A detachment of the instructor Savichev'. (N. Milikić, L Žanović Families)

Yugoslavs captured from Axis forces by the Soviets and sent to Tula in 1944 for training. Those 'tankists' were followed by two additional groups sent in 1945 and later to the Soviet tank *učilišta.27* Various kinds of technical officers for the artillery, air defence and bomb disposal duties were sent on two-year courses at Tambov, Leningrad and Tula in 1945 and 1946. Communication officers were also trained in the USSR.[28] The training included a two-year academic course which created nearly 1,000 infantry, artillery, communication and engineer branch officers. A long list of prominent Partisan commanders passed through the High Military Academies such as '*Voroshilov*', '*Frunze*' and '*Vistrel*' and these courses continued until the summer of 1948.[29]

Partisan forces. Most of the future Yugoslav Air Force personnel passed through different Soviet *učilišta*, where they received basic and advanced pilot training and other knowledge. At the end of 1944, there were nearly 600 airmen in schools at Grozni, Krasnodar, Engels and Vnukovo. In the middle of April 1945, 1,122 more Yugoslav airmen were dispatched to the same schools, as well as those at Armarov, Chkalov, Harkov, Leningrad, Moscow and Lipeck. They were trained for fighter, assault, bomber and transport aviation. Others went to different technical, support and meteorological schools and even to the higher Air Force Academy. The total number of Air Force personnel that were trained in the USSR in the period 1944–1948 was 2,037.[24] In total 5,100 Yugoslav military personnel, of all ranks, were trained in the USSR.[25]

At the turn of 1944 into 1945, other branches of the Yugoslavian Partisan forces sent their men to train in the Soviet Union. Those who reached the Soviet Union included all ranks of infantry, artillery, tank and technical personnel.[26] Yugoslav armoured units were significantly strengthened by the formation of the 2nd Tank Brigade which was formed from Partisan cadres in the Mediterranean and

In the beginning, nearly all Yugoslavs were delighted that they could be educated in the first communist state. On many occasions, that notion was strengthened by the traditional feeling, mainly amongst the Serbs from Montenegro, that they were going to 'Mother Russia'. But after the break of 1948, some much more realistic memories were presented in the Yugoslav Army media, including details such as scarce food and clothing, primitive accommodation and harsh Soviet drill. To these should be added: getting up early in the morning, long working days and a terribly cold environment, sometimes with temperatures below minus 35°C, which produced serious problems for the Yugoslavs accustomed to a warmer climate.[30]

After the eruption of the Cominform Crisis, Yugoslav cadets stressed the underestimation of the indigenous Yugoslav revolution and Partisan experience as particular issues. The Yugoslav Partisans, mostly communists, felt immensely proud of their struggle during the war but the Russians treated them haughtily, belittled their military achievements and generally acted as if they were awkward country cousins.[31]

3

COOPERATION WITH THE PEOPLE'S DEMOCRACY ARMIES

The idea of a 'People's Democracy' was launched by Georgi Dimitrov as Secretary General of the Comintern in 1936 in connection with the Spanish Civil War. At that time, the term had to describe and justify an anti-fascist Leftist government. Part of the bourgeoisie was included for political reasons, in a 'popular front' against fascism and viewed tactically as a transition to a Soviet-type regime. After the Second World War, this concept was applied to the states under Soviet influence to characterise the emerging new order in Eastern

Europe.[1] Yugoslavia and its neighbours were part of this group of states, despite the fact that the bourgeoisie opposition was formally eliminated from political life at the end of November 1945.

Most of Yugoslavia's borders were with friendly, People's Democracy states – comrades-in-arms such as Albania or Bulgaria, or comrades in a proposed better future, such as Romania and Hungary. Of the Balkan borders, only Greece was troublesome. Examining the Yugoslav Army order of battle in this period, it can be clearly seen that significant forces were deployed against the 'Monarch-fascist' Greek kingdom. Whereas, against the other Balkan neighbours, Albania, Romania and Bulgaria, there was no extensive deployment. The only exception was KNOJ internal security units that were responsible for securing the borders. Friendship with the neighbouring armies was so strong that some Yugoslav Army facilities at the borders were closed, for example on the border with Romania, because no hostilities were expected.

It is important to note that Tito, after the successful revolutionary drive which swept him into power, extended his ambitions beyond the borders of the pre-1941 Kingdom of Yugoslavia. This produced bitter relations with the Allies concerning the problems around the city of Trieste (which had been annexed by Italy after the First World War) and the definition of new Yugoslav-Italian borders. However, Tito clearly wanted to be regarded as the leader of the Balkans. Ideas of confederation with Bulgaria, Albania possibly joining the Yugoslav federation and political or military assistance to Greek communists in the Greek Civil War, were all elements in his foreign policy between 1945 and 1948. Many of Tito's ideas and actions beyond his Yugoslav 'format' raised the suspicions of Moscow and Stalin in particular.

Assistance to the Albanian Army

In the period between 1945 and 1948, the most intensive mutual relationship was between the Yugoslav and the Albanian armies. The cooperation between two former Partisan/communist armies started during the late stages of the war. Sometime after the formal end of hostilities, there were still several Albanian units in Yugoslavia. In western Macedonia, there were the 5th and 6th Albanian infantry divisions, who remained there to hunt various Albanian nationalist or anti-communist bands until December 1945.[2]

Even though cooperation between the two armies started in 1945, it expanded in 1946 and continued until the Cominform Crisis. In this period, an agreement of friendship and mutual assistance was signed between the two states in Tirana on 9 July 1946.[3] One of the most important plans for the Albanian regime, was the creation of its own proficient army. The Yugoslav Army had much more experience and it was willing to support the Albanian Army with advice, armaments and equipment. Several meetings of both General Staffs occurred in this period. It was decided that the model of the Yugoslav Army organisation should be adopted in Albania, too. This included the system of mobilisation and training but also different technical manuals and handouts (many of them in fact, translated Soviet ones). Numerous specialised teams were sent to Albania to share their experience and provide additional help to their Albanian brothers-in-arms.

Relations between the two General Staffs were very open and friendly. Meetings were held at Belgrade or Tirana. During the summer of 1947, several important talks between representatives of the two armies were organised. There were negotiations on the further development of the Albanian air bases. Also, a staff military exercise was agreed. This staff exercise was conducted by two the Chiefs of Staff, Generals Koča Popović and Mehmet Shehu.[4] Several ideas about mutual operations in any future war were proposed and the Yugoslavs provided the Albanian General Staff with the latest operational and tactical plans. For example, General Shehu insisted that firm and realistic strategies should be worked out in case the 'Monarch-fascist' Greeks attacked Albania. Shehu was insisting that the Yugoslav Army should assist the Albanian defence.[5] The Albanian General Panaiot Plaku, who deserted to Yugoslavia in the

Albanian communist leader and General Secretary of the Albanian Communist Party Enver Hoxha wearing the Yugoslav Order of People's Hero, which he received in Belgrade in 1946. (Medija Centar Odbrana)

Marshal Tito and Enver Hoxha salute during a ceremony at Zemun/Belgrade airport, 1946. (Medija Centar Odbrana)

late 1950s, also testified to this cooperation at the highest level in his memoirs.[6]

Besides the advisory group with the Albanian General Staff, dozens of other teams and advisors were present for longer or shorter periods to help the Albanians in various matters such as the founding of a communications network, reconnaissance, army intelligence, artillery, technical, support, financial and other services.[7] By the beginning of 1948, the head of all Yugoslav military cooperation missions was General Kupresanin. He had several experienced Partisan colonels with him to provide other kinds of assistance to the Albanians. For example, Colonel Safet Filipovic a 'man with a lot of theoretical knowledge' was ordered to provide a link for the two state security services.[8]

The Yugoslav Army supplied the Albanian Army with various armaments and equipment. There were artillery pieces ranging from 20mm to 150mm, mortars, anti-aircraft guns from 20mm to 88mm calibre and other artillery equipment.[9] Nearly 900 vehicles obtained through UNRRA and from French surplus stocks arrived in Albania, many on Yugoslav ships.[10] Other assistance included all kinds of mines, ammunition, dynamite, engineer equipment, uniforms, food, various manuals, cyphers and codes, maps, medicine and medical treatments for Yugoslav hospitals and convalescent homes. Some of the armaments, vehicles and equipment continued to be delivered until May 1948, after the Cominform Crisis had already begun.[11]

The establishment of the Albanian armoured units is a good example of the level of cooperation between the two armies. It was negotiated that Albania would receive surplus, captured Axis fighting vehicles from the Yugoslav inventory. Those were overhauled and then transferred to Albania. There were over 100 vehicles including tanks, self-propelled guns and other support vehicles. The commanders of the Yugoslav armoured units ordered that those men who escorted this transport should remain in Albania, to train its personnel on the provided equipment. Yugoslav tankmen remained for six months in Albania, providing knowledge and leading the establishment of the Albanian armoured units.[12] The same practice was also carried out with the Albanian Navy; the Yugoslavs provided various support including three mine sweepers and minelayers.[13]

An important part of the assistance to the Albanian Army was the training of its cadets in Yugoslav Army military schools. A total of 470 Albanians graduated from various schools and courses until the summer of 1948.[14] For example, the Yugoslav Air Force Academy at Pančevo had 42 Albanian cadets in five of its pilot classes, the last started training in March 1948.[15] For 22 cadets of the Air Force Technical Academy, assessment reports given later by their Yugoslav colleagues remained in the archives.[16] The Tank Academy in Bela Crkva, had two groups of 60 Albanian cadets in two of its classes. The School for Infantry Officers in Sarajevo had nine Albanian cadets, from December 1947 onward.[17]

An air link was established between Tirana and Belgrade in 1946, provided by the Yugoslav 1st Transport Regiment flying Li-2 and Ju-52 transports.[18] During the whole period of cooperation, only a single Yugoslav Army unit was based in Albania. Following requests by the Albanian General Staff, who were afraid of the developments in Greece, where civil war raged, Yugoslavs sent the 113th Fighter Regiment, equipped with Soviet Yak-3 fighters. This regiment reached Albania in mid-June 1947. Its eskadrilas were deployed to Gjirokaster, Korce and Tirana. Logistical and technical support was provided by Yugoslav cargo aircraft which established a link with 113th Regiment's home base at Skoplje. Albanian rations were barely adequate, so supplies and field kitchens from Yugoslavia were sent to improve the conditions of the regiment. Yugoslav pilots patrolled in the Albanian skies, protecting it from the Royal Greek Air Force. After three months spent in Albania, the 113th Regiment returned to Skoplje on 21 September 1947.[19]

In the period between the summer of 1945 and the summer of 1948, a total of 704,791,000 dinars was spent from the Yugoslavian state budget to fulfil Albanian military requirements,. As well as the huge amounts of weapons, from pistols to tanks and ships, the Yugoslav Army also occasionally sent food supplies, with an estimated value of 3,750,000 dinars.[20]

'We were in Albania at every position', Arso Milatović, one of the senior Yugoslav UDBA officials admitted later. Albanian General Plaku said of the cooperation between the two armies and states between 1945 and 1948: 'We were so friendly, more like brothers than two states had ever been'.[21]

Support to the Greek Communist Army

The northern borders of Greece with Albania, Yugoslavia and Bulgaria were an unsecured region crossed by various trespassers; the remains of various Albanian political or robber bands, the Macedonian revolutionary groups, supporters of the Bulgarian Tsarist regime and their collaborators in Macedonia, as well as members of the defeated Yugoslav Homeland Army of General Mihailović and finally, the Greek communists. All mentioned were trying to reach safety in opposite countries. The units of the Yugoslav 5th Army and the 8th Division (KNOJ) had a hard time trying to prevent these numerous illegal border crossings.[22] Yugoslav troops continuously moved all over Macedonia, Kosovo and Metohija province in attempts to prevent the movement of such groups, as well as to respond to any hostilities with the Royal Greek Army in the border areas. One of these areas was south of Bitolj, on 4 May 1945, involving the 9th Macedonian Brigade on the Yugoslav side.[23] On 25 May, the Yugoslav 41st Division sent orders to its subordinated brigades to establish a defensive line in the Vardar River valley against expected Greek attacks.[24]

The beginning of the Greek Civil War in the spring of 1946, marked the outbreak of hostilities. Military cooperation between Yugoslavia and the Greek communists, established during the Second World War, would follow the flow of the Civil War. The leaders of the Greek communists were often guests in Yugoslavia. Tito personally informed the Greek communist leader Zachariadis on the 'most acceptable conception of armed struggle', even in March 1946. Those talks were followed by the visit of Markos Vafiadis, future general and leader of the Greek Communist Army. He had serious talks with the Yugoslav Minister of the Interior, Aleksandar Ranković, in which they planned further military aid to Vafiadis' Army. A final agreement was made on 8 April 1946, when Tito personally drove Vafiadis around Belgrade. From October 1946, the Yugoslavs were involved in close cooperation with the communist Greek Democratic Army.[25]

This cooperation was correctly defined later by Edvard Kardelj as: 'The help to the Greek uprising was of the kind, that any revolutionary movement should give to another one'.[26] Negotiations were followed by the creation of 'centres' for providing different kinds of military assistance. The main one was in the ex-Volksdeutcher village of Buljkes in Vojvodina which almost became a Greek colony. There were courses established for training officers and workshops to manufacture uniforms and produce propaganda material. From this isolated village, from July 1946, there were routes established over Yugoslav, Albanian and Bulgarian territory for transport into Greece.[27] The coordinator of this whole aid programme was minister Ranković. A long list of important cadres from State Security (UDBA) were engaged to organise all the activities. It was a sign of the special attention that Yugoslavia and Tito, gave to this problem that the cadres came from the UDBA rather than the army.[28]

The military cooperation to the Greek Democratic Army included the supply of 35,000 rifles, 3,500 automatic small arms, 2,000 heavy machine guns, 7,000 anti-tank weapons, 10,000 mines, tens of thousands of uniforms, boots, medical material, canned food and horses.[29] Wounded Greek Partisans were transported over the borders and medically treated by the Yugoslav authorities. In the period between June 1947 and August 1949, a total of 6,137 wounded Partisans were treated at hospitals all over Macedonia.[30]

Several Yugoslav military instructors were illegally transferred over the border to Greek Communist Army camps, were they taught Greek Partisans how to use anti-aircraft machine guns, anti-tank weapons and land mines. Many Greek Partisans graduated from these improvised courses. For example, an anti-aircraft course on converted MG-15 machine guns was organised by UDBA officer Jovan Popović and was attended by 300 Partisans.[31]

The commanders of the Greek Communist Army and chiefs of the Greek Communist Party usually held their important military conferences in Belgrade. In some of these meetings, the Yugoslav Army and security officials tried to convince Greek comrades not to insist constantly on the delivery of heavy weapons but to continue with a Partisan strategy, spreading the uprising much wider to the south of Greece. In fact, deliveries of heavy weapons were not possible, mostly because of international monitoring of the borders. A UN Survey Commission blamed Yugoslavia and Albania for weapon supplies to the Greek communist forces.[32]

On the other side of the conflict, the Royal Greek Army used armed refugees from Yugoslavia or Albania on various occasions. Many of them were sent back to Yugoslavia to carry out subversive tasks but they also fought against Greek communist forces. Most numerous were Albanians but there were also former Yugoslav Homeland Army Chetniks who were used in paramilitary formations such as the anti-communist organisation 'X' commanded by Colonel Grivas. The British vice-consulate in the town of Lerin was the headquarters of such activities and there were several camps spread over Greece. Nearly all of those camps were closed after a visit by the UN Survey Commission.[33]

Border incidents and violations were frequent in the period of the Greek Civil War. Those incidents connected with the Yugoslav Army require a special study because of their variety and number. Incidents included the exchanging of gunfire, attacks on border posts, troop movement near and over the borders, the smuggling of weapons and air violations. It is quite understandable that the Royal Greek Army were guilty of the majority of the infringements, as they were desperately attempting to destroy the communist threat. Units of the Yugoslav Army deployed in the border areas were engaged in a lot of such actions, providing help to the Greek communist units.

One of the most famous incidents was the shooting down of a Greek Spitfire Mk IX over the city of Djevdjelija on 6 September 1946. The Spitfire was claimed by the machinegun company of the 8th KNOJ Division. The Greek pilot, belonging to the 335th Squadron, was captured.[34] The incident was followed two weeks later by heavy fighting between Yugoslav and Royal Greek troops, after the Yugoslav units refused Greek requests to let them pass through Yugoslav territory while chasing some smaller communist units. The number of incidents grew dramatically between 1947 and 1948. On 13 June 1947, an air strike occurred on Yugoslav border *karaula* (watchtower) No.130, when one Yugoslav officer of the 7th Division KNOJ was killed.

The most serious clash between Yugoslav and Greek forces occurred on Mount Kajmakčalan on the night of 6/7 September 1948. After heavy fighting, a 'certain number of dead, wounded and captured' Yugoslav soldiers remained on Greek territory. A Yugoslav unit belonging to the 42nd Regiment of the 2nd Proletarian Division, based in Bitolj, joined a fight between the Royal Greek Army and Greek communist forces since the Yugoslav commanders believed that the Greeks had entered Yugoslav territory. The Yugoslav unit suffered heavy casualties; 17 dead and three captured soldiers. The Greek casualties were one captured and several wounded.[35] The final 'heavy' incident occurred on 30 May 1949, when a single Greek fighter strafed the Yugoslav *karaula* near Skočivir, the Yugoslav troops lost three killed and had four men wounded.[36]

American journalist Cyrus Sultzberger noted in one of his reports while visiting the front lines on 16 July 1948, that the Greek Army was constantly shelled from the territory of Albania, Yugoslavia or Bulgaria. The artillery of three communist armies was also part of the assistance to their ideological brothers in Greece.[37]

The arrival of the body of Yugoslav border guards that were killed in an incident on the Yugoslav-Greek border in 1947, Zemun/Belgrade airport. The aircraft is a Lisunov Li-2, serial number 7009 with squadron number 10, with a removed civil registration. (Medija Centar Odbrana)

The dispute between Yugoslav and other communist parties in the summer of 1948, reflected the Greek Civil War since the Greek Communist Party leadership backed Stalin and other parties. It was a sincere mistake. Yugoslavia was their greatest supporter and logistical base. The Greek communist leadership, along with the radio station, abandoned Belgrade and settled in Bucharest during the autumn of 1948. After the first reliable news spread that Tito had lost interest in supporting the communist cause in Greece, further developments soon

A heavily damaged Greek Army Dodge 'Beep', somewhere on the Yugoslav-Greek border. (Medija Centar Odbrana)

followed. In utmost secrecy, former chief of British liaison missions with Partisan HQs during the Second World War, Brigadier General Fitzroy MacLean, arrived in Belgrade. He was a good friend of British wartime Prime Minister Winston Churchill but had also established close wartime camaraderie with Tito.

During a private lunch on 5 May 1949, Tito agreed to MacLean's proposal to stop backing the Greek communists and close the border for their operations in return for proposed British (western) assistance in a clash with Stalin. This 'agreement' was kept deeply secret for over three decades until the MacLean report was discovered in the archives.[38] Yugoslavia's closure of the borders with Greece in July 1949 was the final military blow to the Greek communist uprising. Defeated by the regular Greek Army, Greek communist forces withdrew to Albania, Bulgaria and partly, Yugoslavia. The war was over; Tito had fuelled it and finally, finished it three years later.

As a conclusion to this comradely assistance, a famous figure of the (Yugoslav) Macedonian Communist Party, Lazar Koliševski, commented: 'We have fed them, dressed them, armed them. We gave them a lifts over the border with lorries when and if they suffered defeats. After 1946, they conducted the war in the best conditions. We provided them with everything that we missed in our war'.[39]

Cooperation with 'Slavic' Armies

Yugoslavia's post-war foreign policy paid special attention to establishing good and brotherly relations with the Slavic People's Democracy countries and their armies, especially Bulgaria, Czechoslovakia and Poland. The depth of the relationship with each of these three armies was different, based on geographical distance, different interests, previous pre-war experience and relations and finally, the personal relations between Tito and their respective leaders.

Bulgaria had sided with the Axis for most of the Second World War and only declared war on Germany in September 1944 after the Red Army invaded the country. Cooperation between the Yugoslav and the Bulgarian armies began soon after with Bulgarian participation in fighting the Germans troops who were retreating from eastern and southern parts of occupied Yugoslavia. This cooperation was never close. Bulgarians were perceived as the previous occupiers by the Serbs and partly by Macedonians. Yugoslavs (Serbs) were treated by the Bulgarians as competitors and occupiers of historical Bulgarian lands. This wartime cooperation

Flags draped over a building opposite the military parade central stage in Belgrade 1946, showing the still not defined but foreseen, Slavic/communist brotherhood of Yugoslavia, Bulgaria, Czechoslovakia and Poland, headed by the Soviet Union. (Medija Centar Odbrana)

was not so vividly presented to the (Yugoslav) public, compared to that between Yugoslavian and Albanian Partisan movements.[40]

However, in the post-war years, Yugoslav-Bulgarian military relations were an important part of the foreign policy of both states until the summer of 1948. In this period, Slavic unity (*slavjansko edinstvo*) was personified in public as the unity of the three key leaders; Stalin, Tito and Dimitrov.[41]

Units of the 1st Bulgarian Army seen on parade at Banjica Field near Belgrade, summer 1945. While returning from the front in Hungary and Austria, Bulgarian troops paraded in front of Marshal Tito demonstrating brotherhood-in-arms. (Medija Centar Odbrana)

Marshal Tito and Georgi Dimitrov, Secretary General of the Bulgarian Communist Party and Bulgarian Prime Minister, at the welcome ceremony at Belgrade railway station, 1947. During the year, Tito and Dimitrov agreed that surplus aircraft of the Bulgarian Air Force should be passed to Yugoslavia to avoid destruction, upon the articles of the peace treaty. (Medija Centar Odbrana)

Much of the cooperation started in 1946. The numbers of Bulgarian students and cadets that were trained in Yugoslav Army academies and schools, were second only to the Albanians. The exact figures of Bulgarian cadets trained in Yugoslavia are still not known. There are many illustrations of this cooperation, for example the Yugoslav Air Force Academy had 31 Bulgarian cadets in the period 1946 to 1948. Moreover, 60 Bulgarian cadets were enrolled in the Third class of the Tank Academy.[42]

The 1947 Paris peace treaty between Bulgaria and the Allied powers, contained strict limits to the size of the Bulgarian Air Force; only 90 (70 combat) aircraft. No bombers were allowed. After these harsh terms were signed on 10 February 1947, the Bulgarians were ordered to destroy all surplus equipment.[43]

Due to the close relations between Tito and Georgi Dimitrov, the two countries agreed to save the surplus aircraft and immediately after the treaty was signed, Bulgaria passed all of them to the Yugoslav Air Force. The Yugoslavs received a total of 291 aircraft: 55 Yak fighters, 48 assault Il-2s, 89 Pe-2 bombers, 30 army cooperation KaB-11 Fazans, 10 training DAR-9s (Focke Wulf Fw 44s built under licence) and 59 Bf.109G fighters. Six of those last mentioned Messerschmitts arrived after the Cominform Crisis started.[44] This contingent of aeroplanes gave a significant quantitative increase to the Yugoslav Air Force, providing for the expansion of some existing units and the creation of new ones.

A batch of 30 disassembled Bulgarian Army cooperation aircraft Kaproni Bulgarski KaB-11 Fazan was passed to the Yugoslav Air Force. They were mostly used by the liaison squadrons established in 1951 and attached to the four Ground Forces Army districts. Shown here is one of the examples tested in the Aviation Test Centre at Zemun air base. (VOC)

Preparation of a Messerschmitt Bf.109G for a sortie. In 1948 the Yugoslav Air Force obtained a total of 59 Messerschmitt fighters from Bulgaria. Some of them were converted to the two-seat version, known as 'U-Me'. (172. Ibap-Golubovci)

Chief of the General Staff, General Koča Popović welcomes the Czechoslovak Minister of Defence, General Ludvik Svoboda, Zemun/ Belgrade airport, 1947. And vice versa, General Popović with members of the Czechoslovak General Staff and General Svoboda, observing an exercise of the Czechoslovak Army. (Medija Centar Odbrana)

In compensation, the Bulgarian Air Force received 80, new-built metal fuselages to replace obsolete wooden fuselages on their remaining Il-2s. Planned technical cooperation between the two states, remained on an initial level. The only result was the building of a Bulgarian basic trainer named the Lazarov LAZ-7. It was planned to test this type in Yugoslavia. Unfortunately, due to poor technical performance, a LAZ-7 crash-landed, killing an experienced Yugoslav test pilot. Further production was abandoned.[45]

Czechoslovakia was an old Yugoslav ally from the Little Entente, an alliance that also included Romania and which was formed in 1920. Apart from the exchange of highest level delegation visits, most of the cooperation was based on Yugoslav interest in obtaining Czechoslovak weaponry. During talks held in 1946, Yugoslavia asked to purchase various vehicles. In late 1946 and in 1947, a number of Czech vehicles were delivered to Yugoslavia, including Tatra 87, Skoda 1101 Tudor and Superb, Skoda 256 and 706R lorries. The Yugoslav Air Force obtained Zlin Z-381 (Bucker Bestman) and Mraz Čap K-65 (Fieseler Storch) light aircraft. In May 1947, a Yugoslav Air Force delegation had an opportunity to inspect the jet-powered Avia CS-92 two-seat fighter (Me 262B-1a). One of the Yugoslav pilots had a chance to fly the 'Turbina' – as this type was nicknamed in Czechoslovakia. Yugoslavia placed an order for two aircraft and six spare M-04 (Jumo) jet engines. The delivery was never fulfilled, except for one engine which is now preserved in the YAF museum.[46]

The new Yugoslav and Polish armies cooperated to a certain extent during the period 1946–1948. Fraternal relations were established, military representatives were assigned to both capitals, medals for wartime endeavours were exchanged and some Polish cadets were trained in Yugoslav military academies. Yugoslav-Polish cooperation was marked by the visit of a Polish military and political delegation in October 1946. Poles were the main guests at the parade organised in downtown Belgrade on the second anniversary of the liberation of Belgrade.[47]

Among larger Albanian and Bulgarian cadet contingents in Yugoslav military academies, there were seven Polish and two Czechoslovak students in 1947/48. Yugoslav students were also dispatched to Polish academies. It is worth mentioning that Yugoslav military officials were surprised that the Polish cadets and officers were practising their religion, celebrating certain holidays and visiting the churches.[48]

Yugoslav Army cooperation with the Romanian Army was not so extensive. One could presume that the reason could have been that the Romanian King Mihail was still on his throne and that Tito had a very anti-monarchist attitude. However, there were several friendly

Between 1946 and 1948, the Yugoslav Army obtained various types of vehicles, aircraft and other military equipment from Czechoslovakia. Here are some of the types: Skoda 1101VO Tudor

Skoda 256B lorry

Skoda 706P lorry with mounted 4x20mm M-38, AA gun, military parade in Belgrade Mayday 1949. (Medija Centar Odbrana)

A T-34 tank passes the central stage during the Yugoslav Army military parade organised in honour of the Polish guests: Secretary General of the Polish Workers Party Boleslaw Bierut and Defence Minister Marshal Michal Rola-Zhymierski, Belgrade, late October 1946. (Medija Centar Odbrana)

Belgrade citizens cheer Polish officers, after a military parade held in Belgrade 1946. (Medija Centar Odbrana)

meetings between lower-ranked army representatives. These were usually on manoeuvres or on the various holidays, such as the May Day celebration in 1948, made by both army's representatives on the Nera River.[49] Finally, there were some Romanian weapon transfers to the Greek communists that were sent through Yugoslavia in this period.[50]

4
INTO THE CONFLICT – 1948

By the beginning of 1948, there were several signs that hinted at disagreements and a forthcoming split between the Soviets and the Yugoslavs. Even perhaps a couple of months earlier, tension in Moscow had gradually grown since the final stages of the Second World War which somehow the Yugoslav authorities missed or avoided seeing properly. In the autumn of 1944, when the Red Army was present on Yugoslavian soil, the first complaints about the behaviour of its troops were sent to the Soviet authorities. Those complaints noted several cases of rape and plundering, during the Red Army's brief passage through 'brotherly' Serbia, the inhabitants of which hailed the Soviets as liberators. One of Tito's closest collaborators, Edvard Kardelj, complained to Stalin on these matters in November 1944. But Stalin firmly denied the accusations, claiming that they were just 'slanders'.[1] And on another occasion the fiery Montenegrin Milovan Djilas, had pointed out to Soviet General Korneyev, chief of the Soviet military mission in Yugoslavia, that the Belgrade bourgeoise were comparing these Russian atrocities unfavourably to the correct behaviour of the British officers attached to Yugoslav Headquarters. The Soviets rebuked the Yugoslavs for Djilas' remark but although he later explained it to Stalin himself, he was never forgiven.[2]

Training programmes for Yugoslavian military personnel in the Soviet Union caused several instances of severe mutual misunderstandings. The Soviets were also making a systematic attempt to plant intelligence agents in the Yugoslav Army and in the security services. It seems altogether possible that the Yugoslavs would have freely given much of the information if the Soviets had simply asked for it. Instead, they tended to recruit Yugoslavs in the classical way, to serve them as agents. The Soviets began such recruitment among the personnel of the Yugoslav combat units formed in the Soviet Union during the war.[3]

There was a huge Soviet effort to try to persuade the Yugoslavs to abandon their attempt of promoting an independent course. A total of 342 officers and cadets decided to stay in the Soviet Union, while the rest of them (1,082) returned home. It was a serious warning for the Yugoslav military commanders: almost one-quarter of the personnel decided not to follow the course of 'Tito and the Party'. It was also an alarming development for the KOS and UDBA to react to. Many of the 1,020 military personnel (as later estimated by Yugoslav Army security) who were enlisted to be informants of Soviet intelligence, were recruited while they were trained in the USSR.[4]

The Yugoslav Government has published a few statements and 'confessions' by officers whom Soviet intelligence allegedly approached in the USSR while they were attending Soviet military academies. Those statements were collected immediately after the Soviet Advisors abandoned Yugoslavia and indicated the full scale of Soviet spy recruitment. Major General Gajo Vojvodić made a statement from which could clearly be seen that at the end of the training of his group at the 'Voroshilov' Military Academy, a Soviet lieutenant colonel personally asked each of the course participants to correspond with him about Yugoslav military problems, based on mutual communist comradeship. Vojvodić wrote that one of his colleagues, being asked by other Yugoslavs what was going on, while leaving the office of the Soviet officer, replied: 'Ma vrbuje, ali

Marshal Tito was mistakenly perceived by the Soviet leadership as one of the many leaders in the emerging 'communist world' after 1945. Seen here at one of the military parades that were held in Belgrade during 1946, his posture clearly shows that he saw himself as the undisputed leader in Yugoslavia. (Medija Centar Odbrana)

nevesto!' (He is trying to recruit me but very clumsily). General Ante Banina remembered that his Yugoslav class, in the same academy in September 1945, was put under pressure to supply intelligence by a lieutenant colonel from the Soviet General Staff.[5]

Another very indicative case was an order to Yugoslav cadets, who were attending various Soviet academies in late 1946, to remove all photos of the Yugoslav leaders from the walls of their quarters. It was immediately followed by the prohibition of all meetings and work of the Yugoslav Communist Party and its Communist Youth Organisation cells. The explanation given to confused Yugoslavs was that in the Soviet Union only one party existed and that others were not allowed to be active. Yugoslav cadets and personnel in many cases continued with their Communist Party activities in deep secrecy and dubbed meetings as sporting events and cultural gatherings.[6] Such pressure on the Yugoslav Communist Party organisations in the Soviet Union was noted but until the break with the Soviets, there were no serious analyses of this practice as unusual or belligerent.

The Yakovlev Yak-9P was the most modern piston-engined fighter purchased from the Soviet Union in the early months of 1948. Two fighter regiments were equipped a with total of 40 examples. Here, a four-ship patrol of the 112th (117th) Fighter Regiment flies over the Brioni archipelago, where Tito had established his long-lasting residence. (M. Micevski)

The Challenges of 1948: Misunderstanding and Break Up

At the beginning of 1948, a high-ranking delegation of the Yugoslav Army went to Moscow to negotiate further military assistance and deliveries. The Yugoslav plans for rearmament were very ambitious and projected a large army. The Soviets were especially irritated with the plans for the development of the Yugoslav Navy and the continuous Yugoslav insistence on the supply of Soviet jet fighters. The meeting was held in a tense atmosphere of sudden, Soviet open distrust, which prolonged negotiations and with no agreement on further deliveries at the end of the gathering. Colonel General Ulepič, commander of the Yugoslav Air Force remembered that,

after the Yugoslavs insisted on deliveries of jet fighters, the Soviet Minister of Defence said loudly: 'Pust shumit nad Belgradom!' (Let it thunder over Belgrade!) which to the Yugoslavs sounded like a positive answer to their wishes. However, the political break started soon after the delegation returned to Belgrade.[7]

The other problem which emerged during this period, was Yugoslav cooperation with Albania. During January 1948, Yugoslav and Albanian leaders agreed upon Tito's idea that a single Yugoslav division should be deployed to southeast Albania, to strengthen its defence against the 'provocations' of the Royal Greek Army.[8] The Yugoslav Army activated two divisions, the 9th from Osijek which arrived on the Yugoslav side of the border near Shkodra/Skadar and the 27th from Banja Luka which arrived at Ohrid and was ready to proceed to Korce in Albania.[9]

Generally, such mutual Yugoslav-Albanian defence plans were not welcomed in the Soviet Union, which saw itself as the general supervisor of both states and its armies. In fact, the Soviets became very angry, as neither Tito nor any of his closest collaborators informed them about these developments. The Yugoslavs expected that the Albanians would do so because it was a matter primarily connected with their defence. The Soviets learned about these plans through their 'channels', which made Stalin in particular very angry.

Edvard Kardelj, the creator of Yugoslavian foreign policy in the post-war period, left a note in his memoirs about that unexpected problem: 'Stalin was angry about our intention to send one of our divisions to (southern) Albania. At the time, the Albanians somehow felt, justified or unjustified, threatened by the Greeks. And they turned to us for assistance. We promised them that we would send them one division if they needed any help. We did not inform the Soviet officials, because we were sure that the Albanians would do so'.[10] In a meeting in Moscow held on 10 February 1948 to solve this particular problem, Stalin and Molotov sharply expressed their disapproval to Yugoslav officials.[11]. At the end of this

March past of the troops and cadets at the graduation ceremony of the first class of the Military Signals School at Zrenjanin, in the spring of 1948. Tito's and Stalin's pictures still dominate the scene. No Soviet Advisors but other People's Democracy representatives can be seen on the right, an Albanian and Bulgarian officer are present. (Medija Centar Odbrana)

meeting, Stalin again mentioned the question of military advisors and claimed that they did not receive proper treatment and positions in the Yugoslav Army. Even more, that the Yugoslavs often did not obey their orders and kept doing things on their own.[12]

On 18 March 1948, the chief of the Soviet missions in Yugoslavia, General Obraskov, informed the Yugoslav military authorities that Marshal Bulganin, the Soviet Defence Minister, had telegraphed him to withdraw all Soviet military advisors and instructors from Yugoslavia, due to the 'hostility with which they were surrounded in Yugoslavia'. After receiving this urgent note, Obraskov ordered all Soviet military advisors to pack their belongings and leave for the homeland. It was a total surprise for Tito and his closes collaborators in the Yugoslav Central Committee.[13]

Two days later, on 20 March, Marshal Tito sent a note to Molotov asking for an explanation of what led to this Soviet unexpected decision. Tito asked for a calm review of all possible problems that had occurred in the previous period. But previous links started to disappear and there was no answer. On 27 March 1948, an NKVD officer brought to the Yugoslavian leadership the first of several letters full of accusations against Yugoslav communists. Three more letters and answers were exchanged in April and May, which were a prelude to the Cominform Resolution that was issued on 28 June 1948; which announced the expulsion of Tito's Yugoslavia from the 'People's Democracy' world.[14] The choice of date was also important as 28 June, or St Vittus Day (*Vidovdan*), is celebrated among Serbs to remember the Battle on Kosovo, in 1389. On the same day in 1914, a young Serbian revolutionary killed Archduke Franz Ferdinand in Sarajevo. Someone in Moscow had chosen this important date as a possible symbol of resistance to Tito's regime.

The Cominform Resolution and the Breaking of Military Relations

At the time of the public announcement of the resolution there were 1,964 Yugoslav Army cadets, students, officers and other military personnel in the Soviet Union. General Jovanović, who, as the senior officer, immediately took general command of all Yugoslav personnel in USSR, protested to the Soviet officials that they had not informed them fully about the situation, leaving them with partial information about the dispute. After this note, he was forced to leave the USSR within 24 hours.[15]

One of the 'Džeržinski' Artillery Academy cadets, Ilija Vukadinović, remembered that Yugoslav cadets received the information about the break from Soviet newspapers, while camping outside of the city of Grozny. It was an enormous surprise for the Yugoslavs, since they did not possess any information about the background of the dispute and had no kind of warning. No matter, they cheered the decision that Yugoslav leadership refused the Cominform Resolution and started to dance in *kolo*. Vukadinović was not in the mood for dancing and this later, after his return to Yugoslavia, cost him a loss of rank and military service and even several years in prison spent in the cruellest conditions. Vukadinović's example illustrates the way that the Yugoslavs handled those who showed even a minor disagreement with the policy of strong resistance to Stalin.[16]

When the clash between the two leaderships was publicly announced on 28 June 1948, the Yugoslav Army was placed in serious trouble, in several different ways.

First, all weapon supplies that were instrumental in maintaining and expanding the abilities of the Yugoslav Army ceased. This badly affected development plans for the Air Force and armoured and artillery units. They were completely dependent on Soviet weaponry

The leadership of the Yugoslav Army during the Cominform Crisis: Deputy Minister of Defence General Ivan Gošnjak (right) and Chief of the General Staff, General Koča Popović. Both former officers of the Spanish Republican Army and senior officers of the Partisan movement in Yugoslavia. Popović, being a prominent surrealist poet and philosopher and a graduate from the Sorbonne, is seen here in a rather relaxed position. On the other side Gošnjak, with a background as a worker and young communist, educated and trained in Soviet Union, had a much firmer attitude. Tito had full trust in them both during the Crisis. (Medija Centar Odbrana)

and deliveries due to the very low level of Yugoslavian military industrial production capacity.[17]

Second, Soviet Advisors who were distributed within the units had complete knowledge about the present situation, cadres, equipment, resources and order of battle of the Yugoslav Army.

Third, the Yugoslav military personnel already recruited by different Soviet espionage services to be informants, now became a widespread spy network with strict directives to provide an exact 'picture' of the Yugoslav Army and even to be the potential basis for a possible coup d'état. This threat became obvious on 11 August 1948 when two Yugoslav generals and a colonel, most likely connected with the Soviet intelligence, attempted to desert to the opposite side. After this alarming event, several Soviet military representatives from the embassy in Belgrade – in fact, covert intelligence officers – had to leave Yugoslavia.[18] The war between the Yugoslav and Soviet intelligence and security services was just beginning.

Fourth, in the second half of 1948, Yugoslav borders with Hungary, Romania, Bulgaria and Albania could easily become a 2,181km long front, with the Soviet Army and its satellite armies beginning to take an aggressive stance. Yesterday's brothers-in-arms quickly became today's bitter enemies.

The memoirs of Albanian General Plaku, who in 1948 was a political commissar in the division stationed in Korce, offer testimony that at the beginning of the Crisis, the Soviets were assuming that

In front of his own picture, Marshal Tito speaks to the members of the 4th Guards Division at Dedinje-Topčider barracks on 22 December 1948. Behind him is General Milan Žeželj, commander of the Guards and Tito's aide-de-camp. (Medija Centar Odbrana)

Even at the start of 1949 the iconography remained unchanged. Stalin and Tito shared the same level of worship, as seen here in Military-Political School in Belgrade. (Medija Centar Odbrana)

Albania would support Yugoslavia. The Soviet Advisor in Plaku's division (a colonel), received an order, without any explanation, to abandon Albania. This was the also case for other advisors in the Albanian Army, as Yugoslav General Kuprešanin reported to Belgrade on 6 April 1948. However suddenly, on 13 April, the Soviets changed their minds and ordered that all their advisors should return to their previous posts – again, without any further explanation to their Albanian comrades. The Albanian leadership had, in the meantime, confirmed their loyalty to the Soviets.[19]

Soon after, Marshal Tito informed the Albanian leader Enver Hohxa that all Yugoslav advisors and military personnel would leave Albania. The last two officers who remained in Albania, one as political instructor in the General Staff and another as a UDBA representative, were ordered to abandon Albania after the Resolution was issued on 28 June 1948.[20]

The Albanian personnel who were being trained in Yugoslavia were immediately withdrawn during July 1948. There were 225 in total, in 10 different Yugoslav military schools at the start of the Cominform Crisis.[21]

Albania was the first to support the Cominform Resolution on 29 June 1948. Albanian cadets who were in Yugoslav military academies left for home on 7 July.[22] Yugoslav Air Force officers' testimonies showed that the Albanians received information about the future rift even before their Yugoslav hosts. Several political officers came immediately from Albania to explain the background of the dispute and to order them to leave Yugoslavia. Most of them obeyed orders without any complaints. However, there were Albanians who really felt sorry to leave Yugoslavia. For example, Second Lieutenant Petrika Manastirki: 'on this occasion said that life in Albania is horrible and started to cry …'[23]

Another very illustrative example is that of eight Albanian airmen who were trained in III Squadron of the 113th Fighter Regiment in Skopjle. Once the Resolution became public, they started to prepare to go home. They asked for the return of 40,000 dinars that they had submitted to the First Yugoslavian Public Loan, as had other regimental personnel. Even though their payments were provided by the Yugoslav military authorities, personnel of the regiment collected money among themselves and 'returned' the Albanians their money when they left.[24] Some Albanian students and cadets remained in Yugoslavia, claiming in public that they did not want to go back. One student of the military medical service gave this reason but was later discovered as an Albanian 'spy'.[25]

Whereas the Albanians left immediately, Bulgarian cadets left Yugoslavia a few months later, when most of them finished their

During the spring of 1949, changes were made to the iconography and Stalin disappeared, as seen here at a ceremony of the 4th Guards Division. Tito is now accompanied by pictures of the members of the Yugoslav Communist Party Central Committee. (Medija Centar Odbrana)

courses. This was the case in the Air Force Academy and probably in other schools, where the Bulgarians left Yugoslavia after finishing their terms in the autumn of 1948.[26] Further aircraft deliveries from Bulgaria were also completed in this period. The memoirs of Arso Milatović, who was deputy of Yugoslav Army military representative in Sofia in April 1948, provide the details of how Yugoslav military diplomats were treated in the satellite states. After the Cominform Resolution was published, chief of Yugoslav mission Colonel Filipovic, was maltreated on the border. He left Sofia without any ceremonial reception at the end of his mandate. Because no other officer was sent from Belgrade to replace him, the duties of military representative were taken over by Deputy Milatović, who 'suffered from comrades every kind of difficulty and all inhuman attacks'. For example, he had a verbal duel with the deputy Soviet military attaché, during a Bulgarian Army tactical exercise on 1 September 1948.[27]

Despite the start of the Cominform Crisis, on 15 July 1948, Yugoslavia allowed 30 Czechoslovak Spitfire Mk IXs to over-fly its territory on their way to Israel. This unique operation was known as 'Velveta'. The Spitfires were ferried to the airfield at Niksic in Montenegro and then on to Israel. The first group of six Spitfires landed at Niksic in late September. The others were transferred in mid-December. The last group of Israeli ground crew abandoned Niksic in January 1949. Israeli Spitfires flew from Czechoslovakia to Yugoslavia with bogus Yugoslav markings, while the blue stars of David were painted on at Niksic for the last leg of the flight.[28]

During the summer of 1948, the first outbreak of hostilities at Yugoslavia's borders came from the Albanian Army. They were

The cult of Tito's personality grew even stronger during the Cominform Crisis. The Army was a strong tool of that cult. (Medija Centar Odbrana)

followed by incidents with the Bulgarian Army. Both had been treated as brotherhood armies by the Yugoslavs. Romania and Hungary joined the anti-Yugoslav military campaign sometime later. The new actor in the emerging crisis became Red Army forces stationed in Austria, Hungary and Romania. In the words of Edvard Kardelj: 'The battle for life or death had started … We mobilised not just the army but the majority of people … Shortly, from the western end of Hungary, the south of Bulgaria and along the border with Albania, all kinds of links were cut'.[29]

During 1949, the Yugoslavian media began to change its coverage of world events. Yugoslav Army official media and sources inverted their view of the world. The 'world of evil' was switched from the West to the East. This process was slow but firm and took up to 18 months to be fully realised. The narrative became that the east was a world of treachery, a world of repression and a lack of freedom and that the satellite states were being exploited by the Soviet Union. This media-projected world scene was a very important argument for strengthening the Yugoslav resistance to the Soviets and Stalin.[30] In the spring of 1949, pictures of Stalin disappeared from the walls of Yugoslav military buildings.[31]

Combating 'The Interior Enemy' in Army Ranks
While the dispute with the Soviets was in its phase of exchanging letters (March–June 1948) and hidden from the broader public, the Central Committee of the Yugoslav Communist Party had been acquainted with the subject since the arrival of the first letter from Moscow. In the Army, the highest circles of the Ministry of People's Defence and the General Staff were also informed of the Soviet accusations and the Yugoslav response in several meetings.[32] However, Communist Party cells inside the Army were not informed about the coming dispute and were not prepared to take any political standpoint. Nobody expected that the clash would emerge into such a large scale conflict. After the Resolution became public on 28 June 1948, many wavered in their personal standpoints on the suddenly emerging Crisis. Stalin and the Soviet Union were, for many Yugoslav communists in the army, an unquestionable authority.

Both Yugoslav security services (UDBA and KOS) knew of the approaching clash almost a month and a half before it became public. Communist Party members of the KOS were acquainted with the dispute on 11 May 1948.[33] To the Yugoslav security services, the coming dispute with Moscow came as a sudden blow. Not just because yesterday's brothers-in-arms now became the enemy or because both services were rooted in Soviet experience,

methodology, practice and training, but because they now had to monitor their colleagues and friends even more. Many security service personnel also had mixed feelings on the dispute.[34]

Both security services joined their efforts together with the Party organisation within the army to combat all pro-Stalin or pro-Soviet activities in Yugoslavia. It was difficult to establish full control of the officer corps within the army. The KOS had the difficult task of controlling the behaviour of numerous army personnel who had been trained in the Soviet Union, ranging from NCOs and cadets to generals. A group of generals and high-ranking colonels that had arrived in May 1948 and were finishing their course at the Soviet High Military Academy Voroshilov, did not know anything of the dispute. They were sent on 'holiday' to Lake Bled and to Sveti Štefan on the coast of Montenegro until their personal standpoint was cleared. Some of 'Voroshilovci' had to be persuaded by Deputy Minister of Defence General Gošnjak or Minister of Interior Ranković, who was also the organisational secretary of the party, to accept the Party position. Some authors claim that Tito personally talked with the 'six most ardent' believers in the Soviet accusations at Brdo Castle near Kranj.[35] It appeared that the Yugoslav Army's highest circle was loyal and this was confirmed at the V Congress of the Yugoslav Communist Party in late July 1948.[36]

However suddenly, on the afternoon of 12 August 1948, a major incident occurred. In an attempt to desert over the Romanian

Tito and Minister of Interior Aleksandar Ranković, receiving the leadership of the State Security Service – UDBA. (Medija Centar Odbrana)

Prominent members of the service who distinguished themselves in the clash with 'foreign and interior enemies', Belgrade 13 May 1949. (Medija Centar Odbrana)

borders, a former Chief of the General Staff, General Arso Jovanović was killed. Two of his companions in this endeavour, General Petričević, Deputy Chief of the Political Department and Colonel Dapčević, brother of Deputy Chief of the General Staff were arrested.[37] Four days later, newly promoted General Pero Popivoda took a light PO-2 aircraft from Belgrade/Zemun airport and deserted to Romania.[38] It was sign that the highest echelons of the regime still had doubts about the dispute and that the watchfulness of both security services should be at the highest level. If such prominent figures of the army and the Communist Party decided to desert to Stalin's side, what might the lower levels do?

It is important to note that in 1947, the 'Guidelines for investigation work' of the UDBA were approved by the Minister of Interior, Ranković. These guidelines enabled UDBA officials to take police measures; arresting, questioning and further investigating the people which fell into its hands. The UDBA was allowed to open dossiers with case details for each suspected individual.[39] It was the same for the KOS inside the military.

Until the end of 1948, there were 2,477 'istupanja' (loosely translated as 'appearances') in favour of the Resolution and other means of support to the Soviet/Stalinist cause inside the Yugoslav Army.[40] It was a significant number and with

Photos of the inmates or life at the Goli Otok camp are almost nonexistent. Shown here are two groups of them, far from the island but still in captivity after they finished their 'volunteer work' in the spring of 1950. The first group at the Kreka mines and the second, showing a group on a train which transported them to the coke (coal) factory in Lukavac, both in Bosnia. (Medija Centar Odbrana)

a trend that did not reduce, as cases were often transformed from focusing on individuals to organised groups with various attitudes; from commenting on the political issues at party meetings, to organising serious actions. Despite arrests, demobilisation or transfers to disciplinary battalions, opposition to the Yugoslav Party course remained a serious problem in the period between 1949 and 1951.

The growing number of pro-Stalin or pro-Soviet individuals who were arrested in late 1948 and in the first half of 1949, led to the creation of a dedicated detention camp. According to some statements of Federal UDBA members, the first idea was to use a converted women's prison in Požarevac, in north-eastern Serbia.

However, after a group of non-political inmates managed to escape from this prison, the decision was made that the camp should be elsewhere in a more remote area. The suggestion was that the camp should be organised on some of the isolated islands in the Adriatic Sea.[41] Goli Otok (The Naked Island) in the North Adriatic was chosen. Construction work started during the first half of 1949.[42] The first group of inmates, Cominform supporters (Informbirovci), reached the island on 9 July 1949.[43] It was the Federal UDBA which was tasked to run this camp, which became notorious for the atrocities carried out to the prsioners. It was known as the Marmor Enterprise (Preduzeće Mermer) or under the conspirative number VP 3234.[44] There were other prisons or camps for those who supported

Tito welcomes minister Ranković and the leadership of the UDBA who came to pay him a visit for his birthday, May 1952. UDBA senior leadership still wore military uniforms. This service was demilitarised in 1952. (A. Ranković Family)

This article was a kind of introduction to what Minister Ranković said at the Plenum criticising 'his child' the UDBA, saying that it should 'not stand above the government or above the laws'. He criticised the policy of arrests, stating that '47 percent of arrests in Yugoslavia in 1949 were unjustified …' and also the tendency of the UDBA to take over the responsibilities of other institutions in society.[50] This was an unusual event; the founder and head of the service posing a strong critique on its activities. This process led to the abandonment of some earlier practices that the UDBA had used in combating the Cominform suspects.

Ranković's criticism was a pretext for the structural change of the UDBA in 1952. On 26 June 1952, Ranković publicly stated that the UDBA was 'converted to a civil formation'. That meant a transfer from the Ministry of Defence to the Ministry of Interior and the abolition of military ranks and uniforms for its members. This was confirmed with an order from Tito on 25 October.[51] The 1953 budget of the UDBA remained part of the Ministry of Defence's budget but following the constant complaints of the army high command, it finally transferred to federal and republic ministries of the interior in 1954.[52]

the Cominform or were accused of it, such as Stara Gradiška prison or the military barracks in Bileća. Some of *Informbirovci* passed through several of these camps during their prison sentences.[45]

The army personnel who were convicted usually took the following terrible journey; Banjica barracks in Belgrade for interrogation and formal sentencing, then Stara Gradiška prison, followed by the Goli Otok camp and then, if they remained ideologically incorrigible, they proceeded to Bileća barracks. Those who relented and openly 'criticised' the policy of the Cominform Resolution, were usually sent from Goli Otok to undertake some 'volunteer work' in mines or construction sites for some additional period. Every one of the released inmates, prior to leaving the island, was warned not to speak of its existence upon their return to normal civil life.[46]

Although criticised for the existence of such camps by the People's Democracy press (the Bulgarian newspapers referred to 'The Horror of the Naked Island') and mostly reviled by those who defected to the East, Yugoslavia firmly denied the existence of the camps at the time.[47] When Tito re-established good relations with the Western Allies and started to receive military aid in late 1951, there were no comments or complaints from the West on how Yugoslavia handled the Stalinist opposition.

The visit to Goli Otok in late 1951, of Minister Ranković, his deputy, Stefanović and other UDBA and party officials, led to some improvement in the living standards of the prisoners.[48] Further changes were advertised before the IV Plenum of the Central Committee of the Yugoslav Communist Party in an article written by General Bajković, assistant to the Federal Ministry of the Interior, published in the party magazine 'The Communist' (*Komunist*).[49]

Despite Ranković's criticism of the UDBA, Goli Otok camp remained the destination of all the *Informbirovci* until the end of the Cominform Crisis. An initiative of the new Federal Ministry of Interior, Stefanović explained to the Council for Interior Policy of the Federal Government on 25 June 1953, that the 'question of usage of the protective measure of sending to a place named 'Mermer' should be revised. Since the number of those individuals which opted for the Cominform (Soviets) was in decline'. It was the first step to changing Goli Otok to a regular prison.[53]

Official KOS figures stated that in the period between 1948 and 1952, military courts sentenced a total of 2,440 persons, among them 1,982 active military personnel, 293 conscript soldiers and 255 civilians who were employed by the army. This figure included five generals, 1,700 army and UDBA officers and 188 NCOs.[54] This represented around one percent of the whole number of army personnel. The total number of arrested persons on 'IB' (reads as 'I-Be' which was the usual abbreviation for *Informbiro* or Cominform supporters) was 16,288. Of these, the KOS arrested 3,678 and the rest were carried out by the UDBA.[55]

5

CLASHES ON THE BORDERS AND YUGOSLAV DEFENCE PREPARATIONS

Yugoslav Defence Planning

Yugoslav defence preparations for the eventual clash with the Soviets and their satellite armies can be traced from the initial moments of the political dispute in February/March 1948 to the end of June in the same year. In February, the Ministry for People's Defence issued 'important regulations for mobilisation and its implementation'. Those regulations defined the system of mobilisation, not just in the army but in civilian life as well.[1] An additional mobilisation plan named 'Star' (*Zvezda*, earlier it was called Adriatic or *Jadran*) would be issued in October 1949 and further mobilisation preparations were carried on until March of 1950.[2]

During 1948, the General Inspectorate was formed, with the task of controlling all elements of combat readiness for the Yugoslav Army. It was subordinated to the Supreme Commander (Tito) and Deputy Minister of People's Defence (General Gošnjak) until 1951, when it was subordinated to the Chief of General Staff. The Inspectorate oversaw combat readiness, organisation and mobilisation through the most critical period of the Crisis.[3]

Until the Cominform Crisis, Yugoslav's strategic assumption was that the next conflict would be a 'north-western front', which meant the surrounding areas of Trieste, on the north-western border with Italy, where the Allies had their contingents (1945–1947) and in the Free Territory of Trieste (1947–1954), which had been created as an independent territory under the UN to calm the disputes over the area. The 'south-eastern front', in effect the borders with Greece, was treated as a secondary front. Despite the long-lasting civil war in Greece, the Yugoslav forces in Macedonia were significant but were smaller than those around Trieste. It is important to note that the Yugoslav Army did not maintain any of its forces at full combat readiness, since the potential adversaries (the Allies, Italians and Greeks) did not maintain such a level of readiness.

The other important fact for understanding Yugoslavia's strategic positions was the reliance on Soviet 'phased' support in a potential conflict. Finally, until the Cominform Crisis, Yugoslav Army commanders counted on attack and frontal combat as the main means of leading future warfare. Defence was perceived as a temporary stage of war operations. The Soviet influence of the 'victorious Fatherland War' and former Partisans' exaggeration of their own strength, were dominant in Yugoslav military thinking during 1945–1948.

Changing political relations with the Soviets and their satellites seriously changed Yugoslav military doctrine and strategy. A 2,181km border with the People's Democracy states turned into a potential front line. Such an unexpected reality turned Yugoslavia's strategy into one of defence. The general idea was to defend the territory from the border areas to deeper into the country, while the mobilisation was organised during the initial stages of the conflict. A further step would be attacks on the flanks of the aggressor's columns, with the general intention to defend the central parts of Yugoslavia as the strategic backbone for a counteroffensive. It was necessary to remain in control of the Adriatic Coast to prevent any landings and keep the links with the (Western) Allies. Full law and order had to be maintained throughout the territory which would remain under Yugoslav control. Such defensive plans led to a large dislocation of Yugoslav Army units so that they could adapt to the new situation. Important factories which produced armaments or other defence-related items had to be moved away from the borders. The building of new armament factories began in distant mountain locations in Bosnia and Herzegovina.[4]

There are later testimonies and indirect evidence that around 1950, Yugoslav military commanders expected that aggression towards Yugoslavia would be a pretext for a Third World War. Such opinions remained and were evident in various meetings and negotiations with the representatives of NATO during 1951 and even in 1953, when the war in Korea was in its final stage. General Pavle Jakšić, who commanded the First Military District in 1951, wrote that he had a talk with the Chief of the General Staff, General Koča Popović, on the possibility of a Third World War if the Soviets attacked Yugoslavia or Korea. Popović was surprised with Jakšić's point that local wars were much more probable than a new world war. 'It is inconvenient that our commanders had different thinking from us', was Popović response, meaning senior commanders in the General Staff or Ministry of

Infantry unit from the Zrenjanin garrison on the march, winter 1948. All the soldiers are armed with the German Sturmgewehr StG 44 assault rifle. (Medija Centar Odbrana)

People's Defence. Jakšić wrote, some four decades later, that after a conversation with Chief of the General Staff, he became aware that there were no instructions on how to conduct a defence, either from Popović or the wider armed forces. Jakšić remarked that Generals Gošnjak, Dapčević and Vukmanović were the most ardent supporters of the defence strategy which relied on the expectation of a world war if the Soviets attacked Yugoslavia.[5] However, all of them were supporters of Marshal Tito's vision.

According to the notes of General Blazo Jankovic, Marshal Tito commented on the actual military-political situation on 6 February 1951, at a reception after the graduation ceremony for the first class of the Higher Military Academy. Tito commented that according to the preparations of the West and the Soviets, the general war may come 'in two years ...' He then commented on how the new war against Yugoslavia might develop:

After the Cominform Crisis started, Tito and the senior commanders of the Yugoslav Army did everything they could to improve the living standards of the active personnel, which meant a lot for them in the relatively poor Yugoslav society. Here, officers and NCOs are buying goods in the specialised Military Commerce Enterprise store at the beginning of 1949. (Medija Centar Odbrana)

The Army was a powerful election machine, despite the fact that only the Communist Party was permitted. Here soldiers of the Belgrade garrison vote in the elections for the People's Parliament, 26 March 1950. (Medija Centar Odbrana)

If there happens to be a war ... for us, there are two variants: that we may be attacked by the Russians with their satellites or that we may be attacked by the satellites alone: Bulgarians, Romanians, Hungarians and Albanians. A Russian attack on us would be a Third World War. In that case, the whole of Europe to the English Channel would become scorched earth. But even if the Russians reach the Channel, it will not solve anything, since they would have to go further. But they cannot, since in the air and sea they are weak, they cannot outmatch their counterpart [Americans] ... So, the second variant is more likely. That they [the Soviets] push their satellites on to us. That would also be difficult for us but better than the first [case]. Since we can oppose all of those neighbours.

Tito finished his geopolitical speech saying, 'I personally do not believe that our neighbours would choose the aggression without the Russians'.[6]

General Jankovic wrote that the Yugoslav General Staff estimated (in 1950) that the attack would be along the whole length of the frontline from Maribor to Djevdjelija:

- On the south-eastern front (Third Military District), the attack was expected from Bulgaria, in the direction of Strumica, Štip, Kriva Palanka, Surdulica and Pirot.
- On the north-eastern front (First Military District), the attack would be aimed at Zaječar, following the Danube River and in the plains of Banat and Bačka. The First District had the task of defending the Yugoslav capital, Belgrade and would absorb the units which would withdraw from Vojvodina over the Sava and Danube Rivers.
- The central front (Seventh Military District) had the task of defending Baranja and Slavonia, using the advantage that the rivers and fortifications gave them. The River Sava was perceived as the barrier which aggressors could not pass.

- In the north-western front (Fifth Military District), which stretched from Donji Miholjac to Dravograd, the resistance would be organised and based on fortifications, mountains and rivers. Here, strong resistance was expected.
- Two army corps, one in Montenegro and another one in Kosovo and Metohija, had the task of keeping the Albanians 'in check'.
- The front was expected to be organised on the following line, mostly relying on mountains: Skopska Crna Gora – Jastrebac – Kopaonik – Rudnik – Suvobor – Maljen – Povlen – Majevica – Kozara – Jastrebarska Gora – Slovenian Alps. General Jankovic commented that it was expected that the aggressors would be exhausted upon this line and even 'feel the anger and contempt of the people' in temporarily occupied territory.[7] Such an expected front quietly anticipated the loss of the cities of Belgrade and Zagreb, the whole plain of Vojvodina and Slavonija and most of Macedonia. However, it also anticipated that the Yugoslav nations would remain loyal to Tito's government, despite the inevitable occupation of certain parts of the country.

General Jakšić wrote of his fears about how to stop airborne landings and the armoured columns and how to prevent parts of the Yugoslav Army being 'taken to Gulags' as POWs. Jakšić criticised the overwhelming expectations of a 'Western intervention' and escalation to a Third World War amongst his colleagues. He commented that Soviet attacks on Belgrade and most of the republican centres would destabilise Yugoslav war plans, even on the first day – as had happened in April 1941, when the Wehrmacht invaded the Kingdom of Yugoslavia. He predicted that the Yugoslav leadership would be faced with a severe dilemma: capitulation or extended Partisan warfare on different types of terrain and with inadequate armament. He criticised the 'shift from the world of reality into the world of fantasy, which was characteristic for Yugoslav revolutionaries', meaning the Partisans of the Second World War. Jakšić criticised various plans which included the flooding of certain territory in Vojvodina, the evacuation of industry into distant areas and permanent fortifications.

Starting in June 1948, considerable fortification works started across Yugoslavia. The most notable works were the building of underground command posts and communication sites. In the summer of 1949, the works were expanded to the Adriatic Coast and in the summer of 1951, permanent fortifications were constructed at critical points on possible routes for invading forces. As the Head of the Engineers Command, General Jankovic remembered many decades later, that it was difficult to organise the fortification works, to adapt the certain patterns or take account of previous experiences. Despite the personnel engaged and the many structures built, the works were frequently marked as unsatisfactory. Several Military Districts and Navy HQs carried out some fortifications upon their own plans and requirements to varying quality standards.

The other important task was to organise the demolition of important factories, locations, mines, roads or other essential infrastructure to avoid their use by the aggressors. A very peculiar episode in those defence preparations was the intention to mine the rocky parts of the Danube River banks to block traffic or an eventual attack from the lower part of the Danube. Some preparatory works were carried out in 1952 and 1953 and the main works were conducted after the Cominform Crisis.[8]

Standard cast bunkers were built at many distinctive positions, even at Kalemegdan fortress, Belgrade (B. Dimitrijević)

Gun position at Kalemegdan fortress, Belgrade, finished in 1953. It could house a single AA artillery weapon, most likely FLAK 88mm. (B. Dimitrijević)

Underground corridor at Kalemegdan fortress, Belgrade (B. Dimitrijević)

Marshal Tito followed by the senior officers of the Guards, inspects the 4th Guards Division units lined-up at Dedinje Field. At the back are the T-34 tanks of the 4th Guards Armoured Battalion. They belonged to the last batches of T-34s delivered from the USSR in 1947. (Medija Centar Odbrana)

Was the Possible Aggression a Real Threat?

Most of the details of the eventual Soviet and satellite aggression come from Hungarian General Bela Kiraly who defected to the West. He was the first high communist military official who openly described the military preparations for invading Tito's Yugoslavia. Kiraly explained that in January 1951, a large staff-level war game was conducted but military preparations started in 1949 when a significant reorganisation of Hungarian forces occurred. He also explained the practice of posting Soviet generals to important positions in the satellite armies. General Kiraly also testified that the Hungarian commanders did not receive a detailed and complete plan for the invasion of Yugoslavia. He explained that it was expected that besides the Soviet Army, the armies of the neighbouring states would take part in the operation, along with a smaller contingent of the Czechoslovak and Polish armies. In Kiraly's words, the main bulk of Hungarian forces and one Romanian Army would attack Vojvodina and create a line at Fruška Gora. Soviet forces would be ordered to capture Belgrade. The other part of the Hungarian Army would cross the Drava River and continue into Slovenia. Romanian forces would attack in two directions, partly in Banat but with larger forces moving into central Serbia, linking up there with Bulgarian troops. The main part of Bulgarian forces would attack on the southern front in eastern Macedonia and capture Skoplje, to cut the Yugoslav Army into two halves. A second attacking echelon, consisting of Soviet motorised and armoured divisions, would attack isolated pockets of Yugoslav resistance.[9]

In his published diary, Tito wrote that in late 1950, Yugoslavia received intelligence that the Soviet and satellite armies were preparing an invasion for the beginning of 1951. According to his notes, the Soviet plan was to be realised in several phases. The first phase would include an uprising in some areas of Yugoslav. This would then be followed by the advance of 'liberating brigades' which would start the battle against Yugoslav forces under the auspices of the alleged 'struggle of the Yugoslav people'.[10]

As many testimonies state, Stalin had serious reservations about every act which anticipated decisive military action, anywhere on European soil, as Serb historian Aleksandar Životić suggests.[11] As Kiraly explained, the fierce American reaction to North Korea's attack on South Korea in June 1950, led Stalin to halt the preparations for on attack on Yugoslavia. Kiraly's thesis is disputed by the Hungarian historian Laszo Riiter, which researched the original Hungarian military documents. Ritter explained that Hungary only had defensive plans developed in case of Yugoslav aggression and after 1951, an attack by NATO forces.[12]

One of the important facts for understanding the satellite forces of Hungary, Romania and Bulgaria are the limitations imposed on them by the peace treaties following the Second World War. During the first phases of the Cominform Crisis, all three armies neighbouring to Yugoslavia had only limited combat capabilities with armament limited to defensive capabilities only. In addition, Albania was, until mid-1948, under close Yugoslav scrutiny in defence matters and its army had limited capabilities, being only able to carry out limited provocations.[13] Even later, during the Crisis, the Yugoslav Army was at least equal in size to all four neighbouring satellite armies, if not up to 20,000 men stronger.

Until the end of 1950, despite increasing Soviet armament purchases and interventions regarding the command structure, Yugoslav military intelligence estimated that none of the satellite divisions was at the required level of combat readiness, even with concentrations closer to Yugoslav borders, the presence of the Soviet Advisors and the increasing flow of modern armament. The Soviet Army in the areas surrounding Yugoslavia, were also modest in its capacities. In Bulgaria and Albania, there were only military instructors and advisors. In Romania, there was an independent mechanised army with three mechanised divisions. Only one of them, 2nd Guards Mechanised, was deployed against Yugoslavia. In Hungary and the Soviet Occupied Zone in Austria, the Central Group of forces was deployed. The main bulk of these forces in Austria were oriented to the west. Only two mechanised divisions were in Hungary and deployed against Yugoslavia. Such forces were significant but not sufficient for making the decisive punch and securing the military defeat of the Yugoslav Army.

At the same time, American military officials estimated that the Yugoslav Army was 'second by size and readiness in Eastern Europe

The Cominform Crisis led to the establishment of the first radar network in Yugoslavia by using captured German 'Mannheim', 'Freya' and Soviet P-2M radars in the summer of 1948. Here, a 'Mannheim' can be seen at a huge military equipment exhibition at Bela Crkva airfield in 1948. (Medija Centar Odbrana)

For the air defence of Belgrade, barrage balloons were introduced. They belonged to the 70th Balloon Battalion of the First Military District. (Medija Centar Odbrana)

As the Cominform Crisis continued, the growth of the satellite forces became evident. They reached some 38 divisions and other units, reaching almost 600,000 men. It then had a serious advantage over the Yugoslav Army, which counted less than 400,000 troops of every type. Maintaining such manpower levels exhausted Yugoslav human and material resources. The CIA estimated that Soviet and satellite forces at the time of Stalin's death, reached 1.2 million troops.[16] For example, in the late period of the Cominform Crisis, Bulgarian ground forces consisted of three armies (1st – Sofia and western area, 2nd – Plovdiv and central area, 3rd – eastern Bulgaria) with 12 infantry, two armoured and one cavalry division with an increasing number of weapons obtained from the Soviet Union.[17]

In general, military intervention in Yugoslavia was impossible without the serious technical and logistical support of the Soviet Army before the end of 1951. By the beginning of 1952, it became much more possible, looking only at the capabilities of the Soviet Army and its satellites. However, in that year the Yugoslav Army started to receive American and NATO weaponry and Yugoslavia received the assurances of NATO that its independence would be backed by force in the case of Soviet aggression. Finally, Stalin's death in March 1953, was a firm sign that the chance of any offensive action towards Yugoslavia was much less likely.[18]

and it can win against any of combination of the neighbouring satellite armies'. The other factor deterring Soviet military action against Yugoslavia was the 'decisiveness of Tito's forces to resist even with guerrilla warfare'. The Americans estimated that between 25 and 30 Soviet divisions, strong armoured forces and serious air power, would be needed for a successful attack on Yugoslavia. Weaker forces would result in only a partial occupation. These estimates dated from late 1949 and 1950. In 1951, the US officials estimated that attacks by the satellites were possible but there was no confirmation of such an intention in Moscow.[14]

Later, during the negotiations between Yugoslavia and US military representatives, there were slight differences in the estimates of the forces available on the satellite side and possibility of their attack on Yugoslavia.[15]

Clashes on the Borders

From the end of the Second World War, Yugoslavia's borders were guarded by the People's Defence Corps or KNOJ. Most of the burden of the conflict fell upon the KNOJ. Its units were scattered all over the border zones and separated into small elements and detachments and in many cases, during their daily routine they had direct contact with 'counter-revolutionary forces'. Because of the peculiarity of their task, the personnel of the KNOJ units had to be carefully selected and they differed from other JA units in that they were intended to be more ideologically committed.[19] Generally, KNOJ personnel proved to be reliable (as their casualty numbers showed) but annual statistics also reveal their ranks were exposed to temptations to desert.[20]

Defined in 1949, the 'state border included the State Border Zone, which consisted of the space 100 metres from the line of the border'. Movement inside the State Border Zone was only allowed to members of KNOJ forces. All other persons were prohibited from entering this area, except for those who were issued special permission. A wider zone was established 15 kilometres into Yugoslav territory from the border. In this area KNOJ and People's Militia operated 'in close cooperation', by conducting a patrol service, setting ambushes, controlling all suspicious persons and monitoring the inhabitants in this area.[21]

Those borders which connected Yugoslavia and its People's Democracy neighbours soon became frontlines. In the period between 1948 and 1954, there was almost a small war on the borders. Incidents included firing upon border patrols, border posts and watches, intrusion of armed groups, the setting of ambushes and attacks on the Yugoslav side of the border, violation of air space and many other incidents. It was later concluded by Yugoslav officials that its army was maintained in 'total tension' during the Crisis.[22]

During the Cominform Crisis, there were so many border incidents that it is hard to comprehensively cover them in this publication. The author has selected typical incidents for each year of the Crisis. They are just examples of the pattern of incidents and the wider actions of Cominform or Yugoslav armies against each other.

1948

Preserved reports of the KNOJ and II Intelligence Detachment of the Yugoslav General Staff show that the first incidents began in the summer of 1948. The severity of the clashes with former brothers-in-arms was still hidden from the Yugoslav public. From 20 July, on the Hungarian, Romanian and Albanian borders, increased patrols and reinforced guards were noted. Romanian border troops were observed with bayonets on their rifles, 'which earlier was not the case', trenches were dug, border posts and some auxiliary structures were renovated or built.

On the Hungarian border, the patrols and reinforcements were also noted. On Albanian borders small border crossings for local inhabitants were closed on 5–6 July. After the period between 12 and 17 July, the reinforcements were noted as well as the manning of previously unoccupied positions. The first shots on the Yugoslav side were registered on the border with Bulgaria on 9 August: a Bulgarian officer fired a shot over a Yugoslav border guard. A Bulgarian soldier standing nearby, threatened the Yugoslavs saying that 'they will see how the Bulgarians beat their enemies'. Firing on the Yugoslavs, began on a larger scale on the Albanian border during September 1948.[23]

Reports reached Belgrade from Albania that Albanian troop movements were noted around Skadar/Shkodra, Kukes,

Puka and the roads that led to Montenegro. Some unconfirmed reports on partial mobilisations were also received.[24] In September 1948, the first Yugoslav soldier was killed on the Yugoslav-Albanian border, near the city of Ohrid.[25] Incidents on the Bulgarian border rose in September. The Bulgarian *Narodna voiska* (People's Army) noted that the first incident on the border occurred when a Yugoslav NCO killed a Bulgarian shepherd near Resen on 26 September 1948.[26] The Romanians and Hungarians began a campaign of aggressive incidents later than the Albanians and Bulgarians. A much smaller number of incidents were noted on the borders with Romania and Hungary in 1948.

During the summer of 1948, Hungarians cut down vineyards, orchards and demolished village houses and other structures to enable a better view of the Yugoslav side of the border. Barbed wire was erected on many sectors of the border and a so-called 'soft belt' gradually was established along the whole Hungarian-Yugoslav border. This 'soft belt' was a strip covered with finely grinded soil or sand to show the footsteps of trespassers. The villagers from Hungarian peasant cooperatives were escorted by guards to the border area to pick corn. Yugoslavs noted that the Hungarians turned one of the largest mills in the area into a distinctive observation post.[27]

On the border with Romania, the incidents came later. The first indications that the attitude towards 'Titoists' had been changed was sudden reinforcements of the units in the wider border area, as well as the deployment of infantry units in the vicinity of the border itself. Up to the Cominform Resolution, Romania maintained a relatively small contingent alongside its mutual border with Yugoslavia. Moreover, Yugoslavs noted that their soldiers carried on their duties with relative ease. Now, the situation changed; fortifications, trenches, barbed wire and 'soft belt' areas were all noticed. The first aggressive incident occurred on this border on 30 September 1948, with a machinegun strafing from the Romanian side into Yugoslavia. The number of incidents rose until the end of the year when Yugoslav observation posts were fired upon. Further incidents extended into 1949 when nine attacks on Yugoslav patrols were noted, up to mid-April.[28]

A KNOJ border guard patrol in a boat with a small dog, controlling the marshes on the Danube, 1949. (Medija Centar Odbrana)

1949

During 1949, the incidents and provocations continued in increasing numbers and of different varieties. Opening fire on the Yugoslav side became usual and People's Democracy states' border guards started to attack Yugoslav border guards. In some cases, the attackers were identified as 'civilians', as on the Hungarian border on 22 March 1949. In other cases, it was regular troops who fired on Yugoslav border guards. In some cases, as the Albanians did, the ambushes were set deeper into Yugoslav territory. Simultaneous attacks were launched as on 1 August 1949, when one Yugoslav soldier was badly wounded.[29] Another border guard was wounded on the Romanian border on 13 November 1949.[30] In 1949, a specific provocation was introduced on the Hungarian and to a lesser extent on the Albanian border – the moving of the border markers. When Yugoslav border guards discovered the changes and gathered to return them back to their previous positions, they were fired upon from the other side. Such tactics were noted in July on the Hungarian border and in August on the Albanian border.[31]

There is a long list of KNOJ casualties on the border with Albania in the period between April and August 1949 – in total, 110 different incidents among them, 27 marked as 'heavy incidents'. Officials in Belgrade sent numerous diplomatic notes to Tirana which offer a picture of the situation on the Yugoslav-Albanian border.[32] Besides random firing, there were incursions of Albanian soldiers and the killing of Yugoslav border guards and even cases when Yugoslav soldiers were taken from their side of the border and held as prisoners. This happened to three of them who ferried Tito's *štafeta* (marshal's baton) over Lake Skadar on 6 May 1949.

Since 1945, at the beginning of May, Tito's various batons were carried all over Yugoslavia to celebrate his birthday, dubbed as the 'Day of the Youth' and celebrated on 25 May. The KNOJ's baton was captured by the Albanians on 6 May along with the three soldiers who carried it to another border post. The official version was that a fourth soldier jumped into the lake to avoid being captured, saved the baton and reached the shore. Fifty years later it was revealed to the public that the Albanians captured Tito's baton and two soldiers. Another *štafeta* was hurriedly made and carried to Belgrade. Albanian forces tried in a few other locations to capture other Yugoslav border guards but there were no other successes. Numerous armed groups were circulating from Albania into Yugoslavia and then back across the border. Some of them inflicted casualties on the Yugoslav Army and People's Militia in sudden encounters and incidents. Finally, propaganda materials, including newspapers, brochures and leaflets, started to be taken onto the Yugoslav side by armed groups or Albanian border guards.[33]

On the border with Bulgaria, numerous incidents showed the 'chauvinistic anger of Bulgarian border guards', as the Yugoslav Army weekly magazine *Front* described it. Bulgarian border guards shouted, 'Down with Tito, Ranković and Kardelj! Down with the Ranković butchers!' Yugoslavs noted that Hungarian soldiers who were digging trenches on 23 May 1949, 'cursed Tito and our leadership'. In the same period, some Romanian officers were noted cursing the 'Serbian Mother' to Yugoslav soldiers. Albanians too started to curse frequently the 'Serbian Mother' and 'Serbian chauvinists'. Old hatreds were now coated with new communist ideology. But the vocabulary was the same as in previous centuries. Besides cursing, there were troop movements on every border and in many cases, Soviet officers were noted as present.[34]

In September 1949, a new form of pressure was noted on the Hungarian border; the illumination of the Yugoslav side by large searchlights. Hungarian border guards had the searchlights set-up at their border posts. They used them to illuminate the Yugoslav border *karaulas*. This could last up to between 10 and 15 minutes. In some cases, they would cross the searchlight beams from two separate positions towards a single Yugoslav border post. This practice was common for the Hungarians in the later years of the conflict. The use of searchlights was noted during the end of the summer of 1950 at the Romanian border as well. Searchlights were positioned around Turn Severin and illuminated the Yugoslav side of the Danube River. The same practice was registered at the Albanian border, in the area of Skadar. A daylight version of the illumination was occasionally carried out by using large mirrors.[35]

1950

The year 1950 saw several military exercises and manoeuvres held in Cominform countries. Yugoslav intelligence noted that Hungarian and Soviet troops held several exercises in areas close to the Yugoslav border such as Szeged, Baja, Kaposvar and Nagykaniza. The Romanians also held exercises close to the border near Turn Severin and Orsava. Bulgarian units (identified as the 1st, 6th and 7th Divisions) also carried out several exercises in areas adjacent to the Yugoslav border. It was noted that the Bulgarian and Albanian Army deployed units to the border area where they built fortifications and carried out smaller exercises.[36]

Incidents on the borders continued. In a diplomatic note, the Yugoslav Government rejected Bulgarian accusations of the murder of two of their border guardsmen on 25 February

A lone border guardsman at a distinctive border post. The photo reveals what easy targets they were for belligerent neighbours. (Medija Centar Odbrana)

The Italian-made AB.41 Autoblinda armoured car was used widely in the Balkan theatre by various Axis formations during the Second World War. Therefore, quite a number were captured by the Partisan Army of Yugoslavia (NOVJ) and pressed into service. Most AB.41s captured by the Partisans were originally painted in Braun (RAL 8020) but after the war they were gradually overpainted in dark olive green, which eventually became the standard colour for the Yugoslav National Army. (Artwork by David Bocquelet)

In 1944 and 1945, the Partisan Army of Yugoslavia (NOVJ) received over 100 M3A3 and a few M3A1 Stuart light tanks. Organised into the 1st Tank Brigade (to which this vehicle belonged), their survivors served into the early 1950s. This example is shown wearing side-skirts applied only after the war. As usual for the JNA, all military vehicles were painted in dark olive green. (Artwork by David Bocquelet)

The backbone of the JNA's armoured formations of the late 1940s were formed by Soviet made T-34/85 tanks. This example is shown as photographed during the Sumadija Exercise, in September 1949, when it wore the hull number 1291 and a slogan in Cyrillic meaning, 'With Tito at the Head, from Victory to Victory' on the turret and 'For People, for Party, for Tito', on the gun barrel. (Artwork by David Bocquelet)

By 1950, the Yugoslavs had managed to launch a limited production of their own version of the T-34/85 in form of the 'Vozilo A'. This example is shown as photographed at Banjica, prior to the 1950 May Day Parade in Belgrade. The inscription on the lower turret stood for, 'Tito, CK' (where 'CK' stood for 'Central Committee' of the Communist Party of Yugoslavia). Artwork by David Bocquelet)

This example was probably the first M4A3E4 Sherman tank in service with the JNA: it was operated by the 121st Tank Battalion, based in Sarajevo in 1953. Through the MDAP, Yugoslavia eventually received a total of 559 such tanks and many of them remained in service well into the 1970s. (Artwork by David Bocquelet)

The NOVJ received a batch of 19 Howitzer Motor Carriage M7s – 105mm self-propelled guns on the chassis of the M4 Sherman tank and nicknamed the 'Priest' – in early 1945. They were used to form a 'heavy' motorised artillery battalion each of the Second and Fourth Armies and, from 1945, colloquially known as 'Shermans' in Yugoslav Service. Originally, all were left in dark green overall but wore the Allied white star in a white circle on their hulls. In 1945, this star was repainted in red – though both colours were soon worn out by heavy use. (Artwork by David Bocquelet)

Peter Penev

This de Havilland DH.82 Tiger Moth (serial NL 986/19) was one of a batch that served with the 1st Pilot School in Zadar, immediately after the end of the Second World War. Notably, it was painted in RAF-style colours, including dark earth (BS381C/350) and dark green (BS381C/641) on upper surfaces and sides and 'trainer yellow' (bold yellow, BS381C/363) on the under surfaces. Sadly, this Tiger Moth had a rather brief service; it crashed while serving with the 2nd School Regiment. After being kept in storage at the Ečka airfield for a while, it was scrapped on 4 April 1946. (Artwork by Peter Penev)

Tom Cooper

During the Second World War, the USSR equipped four fighter aviation regiments of the NOVJ with Yakovlev Yak-3 fighters (111th, 112th, 113th and the 254th). Large numbers of these survived the conflict and served for several years afterwards. Gradually, all were painted in the so-called 'pigeon grey' – actually: medium sea grey (BS381C/637) – on upper surfaces and sides and light blue on under surfaces. In the late 1940s, the upper surfaces and sides of this example were painted in red and it received a white lightning bolt and an eagle (symbol of the Ikarus Works) in white, for air display purposes. Notably, the spinner of the aircraft was in white but had a red star painted in its centre as seen from the front. (Artwork by Tom Cooper)

Tom Cooper

Supermarine Spitfire Mk VC, serialed 9493/93 (ex-JK-360/A) of the 103rd Reconnaissance Regiment at Pančevo AB, as of 1951. As part of No 352 (Yugoslav) Squadron RAF it made a forced landing at Bugojno on 26 February 1945. It was recovered and in late 1945 added to the Air Base Command (*Komanda aerodrome*) Sarajevo, then moved to the III Air District Workshop at Mostar. This airframe joined the 103rd Reconnaissance Regiment in May 1947. In August 1951 it was stored at the Air Workshop 170 at Zemun AB and marked as defective before it was ordered to be scrapped, 18 August 1952. (Artwork by Tom Cooper)

One of several German-made types to have served with the JRV of the late 1940s was the venerable Junkers Ju-52 transport. Enough of these were captured at the end of the Second World War to equip the 1st Transport Regiment, based at Zemun AB. This Ju-52/3M (serial 7201) is shown in the livery in which it served in late 1945 and through 1946. (Artwork by Tom Cooper)

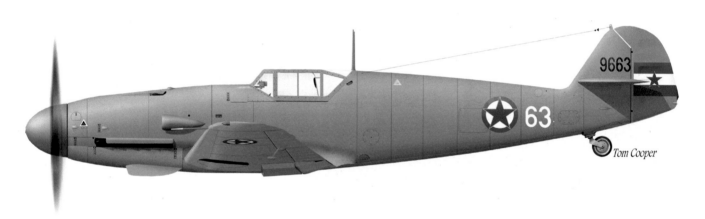

The Royal Yugoslav Air Force used to operate Messerschmitt Bf 109E-3 fighters from 1939, before it was completely destroyed in April 1941. During the Second World War, the NOVJ included units trained and equipped by Great Britain (and flying Supermarine Spitfires and Hawker Hurricanes) and by the Soviet Union (equipped with Yakovlev Yak-3, Yak-7, Yak-9 and Ilyushin Il-2 attack aircraft), in addition to a number of ad-hoc units equipped with captured aircraft, including 10 Bf 109s. On 5 January 1945, all these assets were reorganised into the Yugoslav Air Force. In 1947, Bulgaria then supplied about 120 Bf 109Gs – including this Bf 109G-2a – and 109Ks as a part of reparations. (Artwork by Tom Cooper)

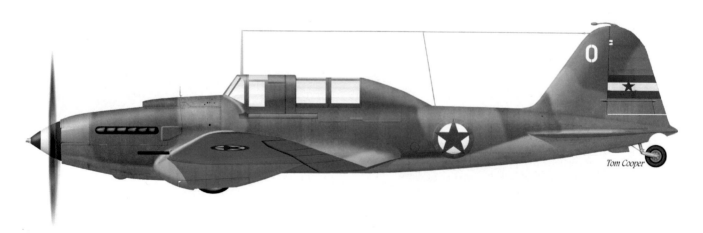

During the Second World War, the Soviets equipped four Assault Aviation Regiments of the NOVJ with Ilyushin Il-2 attack aircraft (the 421st, 422nd, 423rd and 554th). Additional Il-2s were provided in 1945, enabling the establishment of the 3rd Training Aviation Regiment, JRV. Finally, in 1947–1948, Bulgaria provided numerous Il-2s, raising the total of those operated by Yugoslavs to no less than 213. The Ilyushin UIl-2 served with the 421st Assault Aviation Regiment at Nis AB as of 1946. Notably, the spinner of the aircraft was painted in the Yugoslav tricolour and included a red star. (Artwork by Tom Cooper)

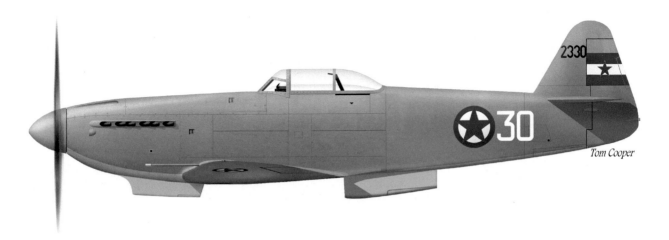

The Ikarus Works began designing and manufacturing piston-engined fighters in the late 1930s. After the Second World War, the factory continued its work by developing the S-49. The type was rushed into production after the break with the USSR in 1948. The first prototype flew in June 1949 and the first operational examples were delivered to the JRV in early 1950. The S-49A was armed with one 20mm Mauser MG-151/20 autocannon and two.5 Colt-Browning machine guns. Most of S-49As were powered by the Soviet-built VK-105 engines and operated by the 107th, 117th and 204th Fighter Aviation Regiments. In 1950, the availability of the more-powerful Hispano Suiza 12Z-17 engines resulted in the bigger S-49C version, of which about 130 were manufactured. Here is S-49A serialed 2330/30 belonging to the 117th Fighter Regiment (Artwork by Tom Cooper)

Starting in 1947, the Hungarian Air Force (*Magyar Honvedseg Repülö Csaptai*) was rebuilt under the Soviet supervision. From March 1951, the force was equipped with over 120 MiG-15s and MiG-15UTIs, organised into three regiments. On 9 February 1953, Lieutenant Laszlo Dombi from the 24th Fighter Aviation Regiment launched from Sarmellek AB, near Lake Balaton, for a training sortie in the jet pictured here. After losing his way, he landed in Yugoslavia. The Yugoslavs transferred the jet to the Aviation Testing Centre at Batajnica AB. They repaired its undercarriage and a wing and then test-flew it. Later, the jet was also evaluated by the Americans. (Artwork by Tom Cooper)

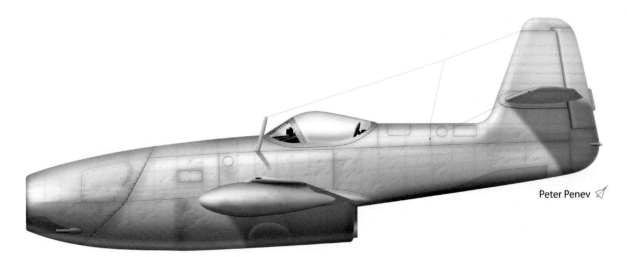

The Romanian Air Force survived the Second World War largely intact but, starting in 1948, was reorganised and re-equipped along Soviet military lines. Correspondingly, a year later, it began receiving Yakovlev Yak-17 and Yak-23 interceptors; 97 of these arrived by 1952, of which 62 were Yak-23s. Furthermore, Romania re-manufactured four single-seaters into the Yak-23DC two-seat conversion trainer version. On 23 July 1953, this example was flown by Lieutenant Mihai Diaconu of the 135th Fighter Aviation Regiment (Karansebes AB) to Yugoslavia. While Diaconu was returned to Romania, this Yakovlev was thoroughly test-flown by both Yugoslavs and Americans, during late 1953. (Artwork by Peter Penev)

On 20 October 1945, during a military parade in Belgrade, held to commemorate the first anniversary of the liberation of the Yugoslav capital, the famous Serbian/Yugoslav photographer Rista Marjanovic took a series of rare colour photographs – even more so because it was the first occasion ever that JNA troops appeared wearing helmets (of German, Russian, Italian, Danish and Greek origin). The first of these shown is a so-called 'flag platoon', with soldiers carrying the standards of different Partisan and JNA units. Red flags belonged to the 'proletarian' brigades, considered the elite of the Partisan Army. (Marjanovic Collection)

From the same series is this photograph of a Soviet made JA-12 tractor, towing an A-19 M-1931/37 field gun (in camouflage colours), as seen in front of the building of the Yugoslav Parliament. (Marjanovic Collection)

A column of AEC armoured cars of the 1st Tank Brigade. The type was in Yugoslav service from 1944 and most deployed as 'anti-tank guns' because their 57mm cannon proved highly effective against the Axis forces. Notable is the 'spotty' camouflage, consisting of fresh splotches of dark olive green applied over the original dark green, that was bleached by years of operations. (Marjanovic Collection)

Photographed at the same time was this M3A1 Stuart of the 1st Tank Brigade. The vehicle shows traces of camouflage that include brown, lightly over-sprayed by olive. (Marjanovic Collection)

Another armoured car of the 1st Tank Brigade that took part in the Belgrade parade of 20 October 1945 was this AB.41 Autoblinda, captured from Axis forces during the Second World War. (Marjanovic Collection)

A pair of M7B-2 Priest self-propelled howitzers, 19 of which were donated to the Yugoslav Partisans in early 1945. They were known as 'Shermans' in the JNA. (Marjanovic Collection)

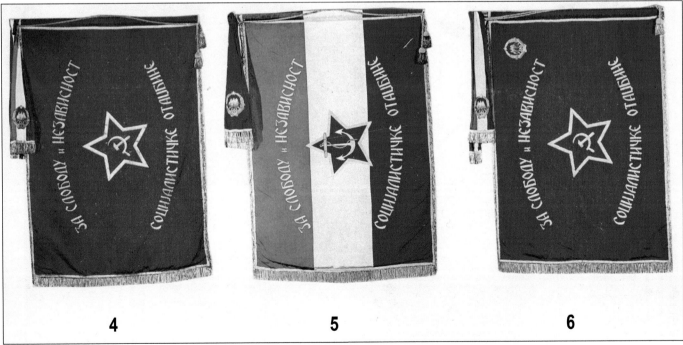

Military standards of the JNA issued to its units in the period between December 1951 and September 1954, including:
1 Standard of the aviation regiments
2 Naval standard (for warships of the JRM)
3 Standard of infantry, cavalry and armoured regiments or brigades
4 Standard of proletarian regiments or brigades
5 Standard of marine infantry brigades
6 Standard of the Guards regiments or brigades. (Author's Collection)

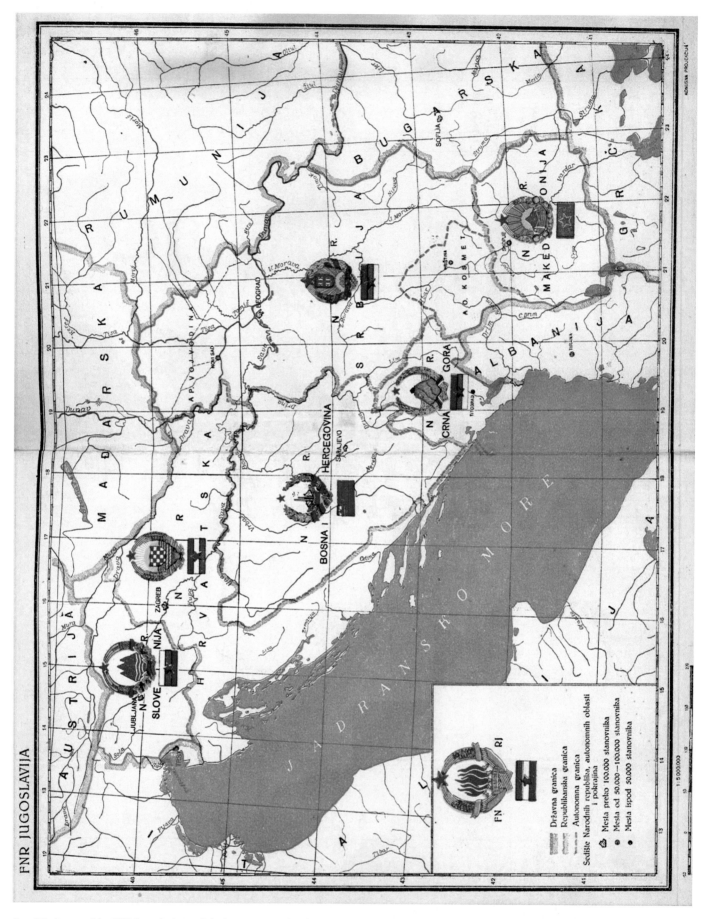

A political map of the FNR Jugoslavia as of the late 1940s and early 1950s, with crests of its six constituent republics. Notable are the neighbouring countries (clockwise), Austria, Hungary, Romania, Bulgaria (the last three were all under the de facto Soviet control at the time), Greece, Albania and Italy. (Bojan Dimitrijević Collection)

1950, near the village of Gjushevo on Bulgarian territory. On the contrary, the Yugoslavs replied that Bulgarians, 'try to hide the real causes of disorder and murders in the Bulgarian border zone'.[37] It was noted that the Bulgarians were also using the same tactics as the Albanians. They would deploy a group of their troops from a squad or two (up to an infantry platoon), set-up an ambush on the Yugoslav side, fire on the Yugoslavs and return over the border into Bulgaria. This was the case on the night of 14/15 June 1950, when a Yugoslav soldier was wounded in an ambush, set in the village of Mazgoš near Dimitrovgrad (Caribrod).[38] In other cases, one or two soldiers would enter Yugoslav territory while the rest of the group would remain on the Bulgarian side to provide covering fire. These were risky tactics. On 13 July 1950, a Bulgarian solider was killed on Yugoslav territory near the village of Klisura.[39]

During the same year, Bulgarian forces carried out several attacks on Yugoslav border posts (*karaule*). Two days of attacks on *karaula* Mazgoš occurred on 14 and 15 June. On 16 June, *karaula* Rovnište was attacked. A platoon of 20 Bulgarian soldiers approached in combat order to the border. After crossing the border, the soldiers continued crawling towards the Yugoslav *karaula*. After an exchange of fire, the Bulgarian troops returned to their side of the border. The exchange of fire continued into the evening. Only one Yugoslav border guard was severely wounded.

Sometime later, Yugoslavs posted a huge canvas with a slogan in rhyme: 'Despite more and more accusations and lies, Tito is loved and dear to us'. Suddenly, a Bulgarian border guardsman appeared and managed to tear down the canvas and run back to his side. The Yugoslavs erected a new slogan and Tito's photograph. Seven Bulgarian soldiers then took positions in the vicinity with the intention to again tear down the slogan. However, the Yugoslavs were now better organised and did not allow the Bulgarians to repeat the action. The stand-off continued into another day, when both sides deployed a platoon prepared for combat but no further clashes occurred.

Carrying Tito's *staffete* (marshal's baton), was an important and challenging task for members of the border units of KNOJ every April and May. Here, an exchange of the *staffete* at a rocky part of the Yugoslav-Albanian border, May 1950. (Medija Centar Odbrana)

During the summer of 1950, the clashes continued, with curses, shouting and insults from both sides. On 4 June, a KNOJ courier was caught between *karaula* No.142 and No.144 and taken onto the Bulgarian side. The Bulgarian side rejected the Yugoslav note on this case. On 27 June Bulgarian troops crossed the border line and set ablaze the empty *karaula* Kopriva, near Kriva Palanka. On 8 July, Bulgarians forces tried to attack *karaula* Deva Bair some 11 kilometres from Kriva Palanka. Thanks to the barking of dogs, the attackers were discovered, the attack failed and the Bulgarians returned to their side. The border unit from Dimitrovgrad registered firing from Bulgarian side for total of 13 days during October.[40]

Bulgarian accounts of border incidents for the same period included a clash near the village of Gnoshevo, near Ćustendil, on 25 February 1950. Here, two Bulgarian soldiers were killed and the Yugoslavs attempted to drag the bodies to their side. In March, Bulgarians noted two occasions of firing onto their side of the border, the intrusion of Yugoslav aircraft near Ćustendil, the incursion of a Yugoslav platoon into Bulgarian territory and numerous exchanges of verbal insults and 'hooligan words

A patrol of four border guardsmen of the 525th Battalion, 229th Border Regiment, Bosiljgrad, seen here with two village girls. It is not known why the border guardsmen of this unit wore the 'šapka' hat instead of standard soldier 'Titovka' service headgear. (Medija Centar Odbrana)

against the People's Republic of Bulgaria'.[41] In 1950, the Yugoslav military magazine *Za pobedu* accused the Bulgarians of taking five Yugoslav soldiers at the border and killing them. The Bulgarians later alleged that the Yugoslavs were killed by their own border guards. In 1951, the Bulgarians even erected a monument on the spot where the incident occurred and threw leaflets across the border, with the text 'Death to Tito's assassins!'[42]

At the border with Albania, similar incidents continued. A group of four men attacked a Yugoslav patrol at Turske Livade, near Resen-Preslap, Macedonia, on 14 August. One attacker was killed and the rest of the group returned to Albania. October was especially dramatic. First there was an attack on *karaula* Škrtac, then on 12 October, another attack on *karaula* Ciganski prelaz where one of the Yugoslav border guardsmen was killed in an exchange of fire and another attack on *karaula* Banjište five day later.[43] Albania accused the Yugoslavs of several incidents; firing upon their side, incursions and violation of Albanian air space.[44]

Rumanian troops opened fire on several locations along the mutual border on 26 March 1950, during the elections for the Yugoslav People's Parliament.[45] Between December 1950 and March 1951 a total of 61 'violations' occurred on the Yugoslav-Rumanian border.[46]

1951

Although by 1951 there was an ever decreasing chance that Yugoslavia might be invaded by the Soviets and their satellites, Tito estimated that the situation on the borders could become very serious due to the continuous pressure from the east and casualties among the border troops. It was almost a small war, in which, as Tito stressed, the Bulgarians were, 'the worst'.[47]

During the first four months of 1951, most of the problems on the border were caused by groups organised in the satellite countries and sent to Yugoslavia. Clashes with these groups and other incidents resulted in a total of one dead and three wounded, Yugoslav border troops. On 23 April, a group of Romanian troops entered Yugoslav territory at Jakšićevo, intending to capture the soldier who was on the watch. It turned to an armed clash and the Romanians withdrew to their side but one of their soldiers was captured. On 1 May, a similar incident occurred at the Bulgarian border where Bulgarian soldiers wounded one of the Yugoslav border guards and tried to capture him. A Yugoslav reinforcement soon arrived and managed to take their wounded comrade to their *karaula*. On 13 June, another Yugoslav soldier was killed on the Romanian border. He was collecting hay with other soldiers from a *karaula* belonging to the border unit in Velika Kikinda. Two Yugoslav border guards (one soldier and one NCO) were captured in July at the Bulgarian border but both manage to escape. The Yugoslav press celebrated these escapes and focused on them as examples of combating Cominform pressure. On

7 August, Hungarian forces attempted to attack another border *karaula* at the common border.[48]

In this period, 1951–1952, Hungarians practised demonstration attacks on Yugoslav *karaulas*. They usually deployed a platoon-size unit which marched up to the border with Yugoslavia then the soldiers would lay down, sometimes firing volleys towards the Yugoslav *karaulas*, or in most cases, just provoking the Yugoslavs to react and take positions for a fight.[49] In Macedonia, at the border with Albania, three attacks on *karaulas* (at Blato and twice at Krstac) were repulsed during October.[50] From July to October, two more border guards and one militiaman were killed on the Albanian border, one was killed at the Romanian border and another soldier killed on the Bulgarian border. In the case of the soldier who was killed on the Bulgarian border, on 27 October, Bulgaria rejected any responsibility for the incident, claiming that the Yugoslavs staged the event and later organised mass 'anti-Bulgarian chauvinistic' demonstrations and gatherings all over Yugoslavia. The Bulgarians characterised the escape of the two Yugoslav soldiers in July 1951 as 'harsh tailored self-praises' – or as roughly invented lies.[51]

To the end of the 1951, 15 members of KNOJ border units were killed on the satellite borders. Three more would be killed before the end of 1953, making a total of 18. Half of them were killed at the borders with Albania. The number of incidents grew during the crisis.[52]

Casualties in 1948–1951				
	1948	1949	1950	1951
Hungary	11	194	342	793
Romania	-	38	278	432
Bulgaria	30	145	204	186
Albania	33	110	112	106

The Bulgarian military press revealed some statistics, as well. They claimed that they illustrated the 'disgusting provocation of the *Titoists* at our borders'. The Bulgarians stated that from the time of the Cominform Resolution until 10 November 1951, there were 285 incidents caused by the Yugoslav side, with 100 after 1 August

Members of the People's Militia seen here during training for different procedures in the border area, including an incident with casualties. (Medija Centar Odbrana)

Typical Yugoslav border guardsman of the Cominform Crisis era. He is armed with MP-40 submachinegun and binoculars. Most likely, at the Yugoslav-Greece border, summer 1951. (Medija Centar Odbrana)

1950. They concluded that the incidents were carried out, 'upon the orders of their masters in Washington'.[53] By the beginning of January 1952, the Bulgarians sent a diplomatic note to Yugoslavia citing 13 different incidents in November and December 1951. The types of incidents were exactly the same as the Yugoslavs blamed on the satellite countries, including Bulgaria.[54]

1952

The main incident that occurred at the beginning of 1952 was the Hungarian taking of an unnamed river island in the Mura River. Hungarian troops did not abandon the island and even reinforced it. In the spring of 1952, many of the incidents that occurred at the Hungarian-Yugoslav border were violations of Yugoslav air space, mostly carried out by jet fighters belonging to the Hungarian or Soviet Air Forces. In this period, the Hungarian Army carried out fortification works, making long trenches or extending the existing ones, especially around the town of Donji Miholjac. In the spring of 1952, Romanians were spotted setting mines in the border area. In July, they placed barbed wire obstacles and during the autumn, they fortified the whole sector from Turn Severin to Kalafat. The Bulgarians adopted a new method of provoking Tito's border guards. They set-up firing ranges near the border with the targets set in the direction of Yugoslavia. The soldiers who were practising their shooting were actually firing at the Yugoslav side.[55]

By the beginning of 1952, most of the clashes that occurred on the Yugoslav-Albanian borders were with the armed groups that intended to cross into Yugoslavia, specifically Kosovo and Metohija and Western Macedonia. Both areas were mostly populated by ethnic Albanians. Clashes were registered around the border *karaulas* near Debar and in the Mount Paštrik area. On 4 August, an armed group led by Adem Duška killed one UDBA captain and wounded one solider of the KNOJ. On 20 August, at the village of Žirovica, a group dressed in what appeared to be Yugoslav uniforms, ambushed a patrol of the Yugoslav People's Militia. One militiaman was killed while three others were wounded. Two days later, another militiaman was killed in a fight with the same group in the village of Ribnica. There were numerous cases of opening fire on Yugoslav border patrols during this period. In return, Yugoslavs managed to capture three 'terrorists' or 'spies' around Tuzi in Montenegro and Mavrovo in Macedonia.[56]

During the middle of 1952, several 'terrorist' or 'spy' groups were sent from Bulgaria into Yugoslavia. All of them were Serbs who had previously deserted to Bulgaria. On 20 August, two of them were captured near Dimitrovgrad, while attempting to return to Bulgaria. On 26 August, three others were killed and one was captured near Zaječar. Two other 'spies' sent from Bulgaria were captured in the Osogovske Mountains in September.[57]

On the Hungarian border, clashes continued during 1952. Tito's *štafeta* (baton) was attacked again. This time on 20 May, when two Hungarian officers mounted on horses opened fire during the passing of the baton between two groups of Yugoslav border guards. Hungarians were seen continuing to construct fortifications and setting barbed wire obstacles along the Slovenian sector of the border. Yugoslavs also noted the presence of Soviet officers in smaller groups who were on surveillance missions at the border or working with the Hungarian Army and 'issuing the orders to them'.

There were several cases of firing on Yugoslav border guards between July and December of 1952, at border posts near Špicberg, Novakovci, Podrašnica, Žitkovac, Središće, Čepinac and others. Hungarian troops set a fire around *karaule* Ljivnik-Mataševac in the night between 11 and 12 July and on 15 August at *karaula* No. 57, propaganda materials were sent to the Yugoslavian side by using large bottles thrown into a river or they were sent by balloons, as recorded on 13 September, 5 and 9 October. Yugoslavs noted that on the day of local elections, Hungarian forces carried out 'manoeuvres' in the Hodoš and Špicberg area. Yugoslavia sent a diplomatic note to Hungary, blaming them for a total of 173 incidents that occurred in November and December 1952. In the same period there were 59 border incidents on the Bulgarian border.[58]

On the other side, the Bulgarian military press illustrates the responses of the People's Democracy states to Yugoslav provocations, real or alleged. Albania protested Yugoslav violations of its airspace on 21 and 22 February, as well as protesting about firing across the border on 22 February. In March, Hungary complained of the incursion of Yugoslav agents in area of Nyisvar on the night of 23 March. Yugoslavs opened fire on another sector for some 10 to 15 minutes to attract and redirect the attention of the Hungarian border guards. In the following month, Hungarians counted a total of 207 incidents caused by Yugoslav forces and one wounded Hungarian border guard.

On 19 April, a diplomatic note sent to Yugoslavia counted a total of 18 violations of Hungarian air space, just in the previous month, which were described as Yugoslav 'systematic provocations'. A Bulgarian diplomatic note issued 10 days later counted Yugoslav provocations on its borders between January and April 1952. These

Soldiers of 85th Battalion, 476th Guards Brigade, taking water from a village spring (česma) at Konopište village, Macedonia, 1952. (Medija Centar Odbrana)

An alert was given at a border post (karaula), in 1952. Border guardsmen rush out to take up their positions.

Taking positions around the karaula during the night. Officer (left) and corporal (right) are both armed with Beretta M-38/42 9mm submachine guns. (Medija Centar Odbrana)

were 11 instances of sending propaganda materials by balloon, six violations of air space and five openings of fire onto the Bulgarian side.

By mid-June, Albanians protested after one Yugoslav aircraft made a night overflight in the area of Lješ (Lezhe)-Flora (Vlora) – the Adriatic Sea, in which leaflets and propaganda material were dropped. Albanian anti-aircraft artillery opened fire on intruder.[59] With the range of available Yugoslav aircraft at this time it is difficult to judge to which Air Force the intrusion aircraft belonged.

Air Incidents

Many border incidents during the Crisis were air incidents, mostly violations of air space. In most cases, these 'provocations' were reconnaissance missions or just incursions to alert or 'to check' the other side's air defences. Those incidents grew in frequency, especially after the Air Forces of the Cominform states received the first Soviet-built jet fighter, the Yakovlev Yak-23, as Bulgaria did in 1950.[60] In the later years of the Crisis, 1952–1954, the Cominform Air Forces and Soviet Air Force (based in Hungary), carried out numerous incursions using the most modern Soviet fighter jet, the Mikoyan-Gurevich MiG-15. During this period, the Yugoslavs recorded the first intrusion by satellite jet fighters on 14 July 1952, to the east of the city of Subotica. The aircraft was in Yugoslavian air space for three minutes, flying at an altitude of 2,000 metres. It was identified as a MiG-15. The Yugoslav Air Force magazine Krila armije assumed that the jet was flown by a 'Russian pilot'.[61]

From this period on, the Yugoslav military press described the tactics of the satellite Air Forces. Aircraft from Hungary or Bulgaria would enter Yugoslav air space and then, while returning to its territory, demonstrative anti-aircraft artillery fire would be opened from its own side. In July, such a practice was noted on the Hungarian border and then, from October on the Bulgarian border as well. During the autumn of 1952, incursions were made mostly by jet aircraft. They even used to appear in two- or four-ship formations at numerous sectors along the Yugoslav border. There were nearly daily violations of Yugoslav air space during the October-December period, as can be seen from the Yugoslav military press and diplomatic notes. There were days when several incursions were noted, mostly from Hungarian airspace and the Bulgarian sector of the border, around Kalotina, Pirot and Dimitrovgrad. In most cases they were jets, usually identified as MiG-15s.[62]

The Yugoslavs commented on this practice:

Hungarians are distinguished by the provocations in our airspace … All overflights were carried out upon the orders from Moscow. Moreover, one may say that these overflights are carried out to a certain pattern. In this period, we have more provocations on the southern borders, while there are few on the northern parts and vice versa. Beside the observation of our territory, it is most likely that these aircraft were fitted with devices for photo reconnaissance. Such facts were given earlier by defected Romanian aviators.[63]

The airspace violations continued into 1953.

Even before the signing of the Military Assistance Pact with the United States in mid-November 1951, it was obvious that Yugoslavia (Tito in particular) enabled the USAF to operate over its airspace and carry out various reconnaissance missions. Starting in 1951, USAF aircraft operated along Yugoslav's borders with Hungary and then with Romania and Bulgaria. In some other cases, American civilian airliners, mostly on routes from Belgrade to Athens, diverged from their regular flightpath to over-fly the Bulgarian borderlands, as recorded on 11 May, 21 June and 13 December 1951. They would abandon the corridor and continue over Belasica Mountain and the towns of Berovo and Kriva Palanka, into Bulgarian territory and then return to their regular route in the area where Yugoslav airspace met Greek airspace. In those cases, the Bulgarian AA artillery opened fire on the American aircraft but without success. Yugoslavia officially warned the Americans of the problems caused by such sorties.[64]

That care should have been taken with Soviet and satellite air defences, was shown by the example of a Douglas C-47 transport (USAF serial 43-16026) belonging to the 85th Air Depot Wing. It was flying from Erding airbase in Germany to Belgrade, carrying cargo for the US military representatives in Yugoslavia. It was caught flying inside Hungarian airspace by Soviet interceptors, near Pecs. The C-47 was forced to land, after which the crew and cargo were captured.[65]

The Intelligence War in the Borderlands

Once the Cominform Crisis started, mutual fraternity disappeared. Besides the 'small war' on the borders, there was also an important and widespread intelligence war between Yugoslavia and the Cominform states. During the conflict, many diplomats and officers of the different services would be expelled from Yugoslavia or the Cominform states.[66]

Both Yugoslav security services developed their procedures and widened their structure and organisation in society. Since the conflict was ongoing for a non-predictable length of time, the federal-level UDBA became responsible for running intelligence operations against the neighbouring communist countries. The intention was to control possible security threats and prepare for an eventual attack against the Yugoslav state and to combat the Soviet and People's Democracy propaganda and occasional incursions over the borders.

The sudden change in Yugoslavia's foreign environment led to improvements in UDBA practice. In this period, between 1949 and 1954, the UDBA developed a peculiar organisational structure of intelligence centres (*Obaveštajni centar*) and sub-centres (*Obaveštajni*

A UDBA or KOS officer with two members of People's Militia armed with captured German MKb-42 and MP-40 submachineguns, posing with a prisoner in the border area, late 1948. (Medija Centar Odbrana)

podcentar). Centres were part of I (intelligence) Department of the UDBA *za Jugoslaviju,* headed by Edo Brajnik 'Štefan', a Slovenian member of the Communist Party and Partisan intelligence in that province. Intelligence centres were the operational units, created to run intelligence operations against Hungary, Romania, Bulgaria and Albania. Usually, an intelligence centre was organised in a larger administrative centre (such as Niš, Novi Sad, Osijek, or Varazdin), while sub-centres were in the towns close to the border (such as Senta or Subotica). The main tasks of those centres were gathering intelligence, propaganda, the infiltration of agents and coordination with the border units of then KNOJ. It was the practice that UDBA officers (no matter what their rank), deployed in centres and especially in sub-centres, had to use different names to cover their identities.

Each centre or sub-centre was tasked with collecting information on the military, security and political events on the 'other' side in its area of responsibility. They used to recruit and insert agents who were mostly tasked with gathering information on military activities, troop movements and reinforcements. Received information of the 'military kind' was passed to the II Intelligence Department of the Yugoslav General Staff.[67] In later phases of the Crisis, the UDBA organised complicated operations to insert its officers or agents deep into the Cominform states, to penetrate their security services or party organisations.[68] There were successful operations but, as can be concluded from UDBA documents, some of those agents fell into the hands of neighbouring countries' security services.

The Cominform states also developed their intelligence networks to counter the Yugoslavs, gather information, distribute propaganda materials and infiltrate agents and sabotage groups. Most of the operations were coordinated by the Soviet services which had representatives present along the Yugoslav borders and in the HQs of the different Cominform security or intelligence services. Bulgarian historian Iordan Baev explains that the Soviets started with an intelligence operation codenamed 'Star' at the Yugoslav-Bulgarian border to establish clandestine channels for inserting propaganda materials and agents to into Yugoslavia. Another operation, 'Arrow', gathered intelligence information on the Yugoslav Army and connected with Cominform supporters in Yugoslavia.[69] Baev also notes that on the Bulgarian side there were no military intelligence actions against Yugoslavia until the end of June 1948. He notes that after learning of the deployment of the Yugoslav 16th Rifle Division from Štip to Caribrod, Georgi Dimitrov ordered measures to protect the Bulgarian borders and informed Stalin and Molotov on 26 July 1948. Baev writes that in 1949 Bulgarian military intelligence organised three intelligence centres, in the towns of Vidin, Slivnica and Dupnica, from where the intelligence and agent insertion operations were carried out.[70]

As an example of the intelligence work of the People's Democracy services, it is possible to examine Hungarian intelligence operations and some of the activities of the Albanian Security and Intelligence Service, as recorded in the papers of the Yugoslav UDBA service.

After the Resolution was issued, the Hungarian security service (AVH), formed several intelligence centres at their district departments in Szeged, Pecs, Szombathely and Budapest. Officers from these centres developed aggressive operations during 1949, mostly using different Yugoslav émigrés but without any careful selection for their suitability. The Yugoslav UDBA concluded that in 1948/1949, the AVH mostly used its agents for propaganda work, inserting the material into Yugoslavia using various means; trains, the Danube and balloons, as well as agents.

In the same year (1949), the Hungarian Military Intelligence Service (VPO) organised their centres near to the AVH centres. The UDBA estimated that the VPO agents and operatives were better trained and prepared for intelligence work against Yugoslavia, 'which was not the case with the intelligence combinations run by the AVH'.

The UDBA recorded that the AVH service was reorganised in 1950. In their HQs in Budapest, a special department was formed to oversee the intelligence work against Yugoslavia. The intelligence centres in Szeged, Pecs and Szombathely were attached to the border units as the 'units for long-range reconnaissance' (Tavol Felderito Ostaly) and the officers of the AVH were now labelled as officers of the border units. In those HQs, the 'units for long-range reconnaissance' were formed to accept the émigrés from Yugoslavia, extract as much information as possible, then send the deserters or émigrés to a camp in Jaszbereny and organise the intelligence activities in the border area. After this reorganisation, the AVH concentrated more on intelligence work and on creating a network in Yugoslavia. They were now much more interested in military activities, especially after Yugoslavia began to get assistance from the West through the MDAP. They were monitoring and gathering information on the new equipment and the presence of American and NATO instructors and/or troops. Among 15 AVH agents captured in Yugoslavia in 1953, 13 of them only had military tasks. In 1952 and 1953, Yugoslav deserters and émigrés were not sent back to Yugoslavia and the choice of personalities was rather different. Between 1948 and 1953, a total of 115 Yugoslav émigrés or deserters were captured as agents for the Hungarian intelligence service.

Some of the émigrés, who were captured later by Yugoslavs complained that the Hungarians, usually with Soviet officers present, mostly just asked them for intelligence on the Yugoslav Army or UDBA, whilst in many cases, the émigrés expected a warmer ideological welcome. On their part, the Hungarians (and Soviets) feared that Yugoslavia was deliberately sending intelligence officers posing as émigrés and so the Hungarians adopted harsh interrogation procedures, mandatory prison time and in the cases when the supposed defector was an Army or UDB/KOS officer, they were usually sent back with a task to prove their loyalty and

opposition to the 'Titoists'. Among 282 émigrés from Yugoslavia that were in Hungary (out of a total of 402 émigrés to all countries recorded by name by the UDBA from 1948), there were eight officers and 67 soldiers – or around a quarter of the total. A further 75 had served as conscripts in the Yugoslav Army or served earlier in the JNA. Half of the émigrés could provide at least some kind of information concerning the Yugoslav Army to their Hungarian or Soviet interrogators when they deserted.[71]

According to UDBA analyses, the Albania security and intelligence services operated in a similar way to their Hungarian comrades. The Albanian border was difficult to control and in the whole period, as was the case in many previous decades, even centuries, armed bands roamed this area. The Cominform Crisis did not change anything, except for the ideology and personal motives of the bands.

The defectors, deserters and émigrés from Yugoslavia can be broadly separated into two different types, both with their roots back in the Second World War. The first type were hard-line communists, nearly all of them Montenegrins and mostly either members of the Partisan movement from 1941 or of the Communist Party prior to the War. The second type were ethnic Albanians from Yugoslavia, many of whom had previously served in various Axis forces. There were also Albanians who had served Yugoslavia but believed more in the Soviet and Albanian path, than Tito's. Now they both had the same enemy as Albania – the 'Titoists'.

However, Albania imprisoned many of the first group, some of them with long sentences, since the Albanian security services did not trust most of the high-ranking JA, UDBA, or KOS officers or members that escaped to Albania. In some cases, Yugoslav agents managed to sow misinformation about some of those defectors, claiming that they were agents rather than believers in Stalin. Many of them were sent to Yugoslavia with mostly terrorist tasks, in smaller or larger groups, to prove their hostility to Yugoslavia. Many of them managed to enter Yugoslavian territory and a few of them were killed by the Yugoslav Army/KNOJ or Militia. Some of the groups managed to kill KNOJ, JA, or UDBA officers, or representatives of the civil authorities. Some of the defectors decided to surrender to the authorities upon their arrival into Yugoslavia, dissatisfied with their treatment in Albania. In many cases, the groups were organised and sometimes led by younger officers of the II Department of the Albanian General Staff. The camps where they were held, were known by the inevitable number of the 'military post'. The defections and activities of the named groups continued even after Khrushchev's visit to Belgrade and the rapprochement of Soviet-Yugoslav relations after Stain's death.

Two serious blows to the Yugoslav intelligence network in Albania occurred in 1950. In first case, after reaching Albanian officials, Lieutenant Nikola Malovic revealed the names of two Yugoslav agents in Albania, one of them an active officer. They were each sentenced to 20 years imprisonment. The other case was much more serious; the defection of Lieutenant Mustafa Lleshi on 4 September 1950. Lleshi, 25-years-old, was a UDBA officer based in the intelligence centre at Ohrid. After reaching Albania, he revealed the names of the UDBA agents and collaborators in Albania, whom he personally knew and handled. A public trial was held in Peshkopi, where four UDBA agents or collaborators were sentenced to death, whilst eight others were sentenced to 15 to 20 years of imprisonment. All of them had their property confiscated. This was doubtless a serious setback to Yugoslav intelligence affairs in Albania.[72]

Finally, after a part of the archive of the Soviet KGB was opened, a story was revealed that Soviet intelligence engaged an agent named Josif Grigurevch to try to assassinate Tito. In this operation, he was named 'Max' and took as his cover, the role of the Costa Rican consul in Belgrade. The plan was that Grigurevich would use one of the diplomatic events, such as a reception, to get close to Tito and by using poison gas at a close distance, kill him. This operation was launched in late 1952 but cancelled after Stalin's death in March 1953 and 'Max' was withdrawn back to the Soviet Union.[73]

6
THE YUGOSLAV ARMY UNDER PRESSURE

Continuous Yugoslav Army Reorganisations

By the beginning of 1948, before there was any sign of the Crisis or disruption in relations with the Soviets, the Yugoslav Army senior commanders ordered a large reorganisation of its forces. The main idea was to organise the Army to counter aggression from the west: Italy, Austria and the Adriatic Coast, with Greece as a secondary front. The new plans also included the whole Albanian Army as a part of the defence. The plan was made in 'Maximum' and 'Minimum' versions.[1] According to documents from the KOS, in the first four months of 1948, this plan was actually known as 'Steel' (Celik).[2]

In this plan, the six existing armies within the ground forces were reorganised into five military districts. The 4th and the 6th Army/ Military District were intentionally omitted to confuse the potential enemy. Military districts became 1, 2, 3, 5 and 7 later losing the 2nd as well leaving only odd numbers

First formed from earlier Belgrade Defence HQs responsible for the Yugoslav capital.
Second formed from the Third Army with an HQ in Novi Sad covering Vojvodina.
Third formed from First Army HQ, which was transferred to Niš. It had to two armies:
Eighth (ex-Fifth) in Skopjle and Ninth (former First) in Kragujevac. It covered Serbia proper, Kosovo and Metohija province and Macedonia.
Fifth formed from Second Army HQs in Zagreb. It also had two armies: Tenth in Ljubljana (previously Fourth) and Twelfth (former the Second) in Zagreb. This military district was responsible for the defence of the western parts of Yugoslavia, in the area where the most serious threat was expected.

Seventh formed by the reorganisation of the earlier Sixth Army, with same territorial area of responsibility: Bosnia and Herzegovina and Montenegro.

The new organisational structure had to start functioning on 20 January 1948. The five military districts, together with Guards, Air Force, Navy and KNOJ were now the strategic organisations of the Yugoslav Army. Two Military Districts (3rd and 5th) each had two armies under their command, since it was expected that the main aggression would be at their areas. They had no military territorial

During the winter of 1949–1950, the members of the sole Mountain Brigade (the 16th, but from 1950, the 345th) based in north-western Slovenia, seen here during a small break. This was the first season when the Brigade adopted their later very distinguished mountain uniforms and caps. (Medija Centar Odbrana)

Line-up of T-34 tanks belonging to the 268th Tank Brigade, in a field near Fužine. On the left side, is a rare T-34/76, a 'beute' or captured tank from the German *Polizei Panzer Kompanie 5*, carrying JA serial 1042. (Medija Centar Odbrana)

responsibilities and had only to take care of the operational and combat readiness of their subordinated units.[3] Two existing tank divisions were transformed by adding third tank brigades into mechanised corps and subordinated to the Third and Fifth Military Districts.[4] Upon this plan, territorial air defence was reorganised into four AA Defence Divisions, with HQs in Belgrade, Novi Sad, Niš and Sarajevo. But, due to a lack of equipment, they were disbanded at the end of the same year.[5]

Unexpectedly, during the reorganisation, relations with the Soviet Union started to worsen, their advisors were recalled and relations with other People's Democracy armies deteriorated, especially with the Albanian Army, which was part of the broader defence plans. The situation was difficult as the Soviet Advisors were very familiar with the plans, structure and capabilities of the Yugoslav Army. A new plan was needed.

The Yugoslav General Staff ordered on 14 May 1948 that all units from divisions to independent battalions should be renamed. The exceptions were three elite 'proletarian' divisions (1st, 2nd and 6th) and the first Partisan brigade created: the 1st Proletarian Brigade/Regiment.[6] The names of the units were also changed within the Navy, where most of the units were without numbered titles.[7]

All five-digit 'military posts' that had masked the real organisation titles since 1946, were now changed into new ones, with four digits. During the summer of 1948, all the units were renamed and some of them already changed their locations upon the emerging threat from the East. For example:

- 554th Aviation Regiment (VP 76517) at Niš, now became the 81st Aviation Regiment (VP 2586)
- 42nd Airfield Command (VP 35143e) at Cerklje, became the 200th Air Technical Battalion (VP 8651).[8]

It is still unclear whether the system of regimental organisation was planned before or after the early dispute with the Soviets. Rifle, artillery, engineer, signals and other brigades were turned into regiments with new titles. For example, the 13th Proletarian Brigade became the 124th Proletarian Rifle Regiment. Some of the rifle brigades remained at so-called isolated tactical locations, all of them in Slovenia or Macedonia. This reorganisation abolished the names of the earlier Partisan (rifle) divisions and brigades with their original, in most cases regional titles. They became numbered rifle (infantry) units. For example, the 26th Dalmatian Division became the 60th Rifle Division and the 8th Krajina Brigade was redesignated the 93rd Rifle Regiment. For the sake of the interior cohesion of the Army, it was necessary that all regional differences had to be abandoned in favour of a broader Yugoslav identity. Security within the ranks became tighter. Numerous soldiers served conscript time knowing only the number of the military post or the name

After the transfer of the Air Academy from several south Banat airfields to Mostar in 1949, its training Aero-2 aircraft were repainted in yellow colour scheme, to be better observed in the Herzegovina rocky scenery. (Medija Centar Odbrana)

of their barracks, rather than the real name of the unit in which they served.

As the Crisis continued into 1949, the Yugoslav Army carried on reorganising and adapting to the new military-political situation. Tito approved a new plan called 'Pearl' (*Biser*) on 24 July 1949. This plan provided instructions for a further reorganisation of the JA units in the period after the new conscripts arrived in late October 1949. This plan had to be completed by 1 March 1950. This date was marked as the start of the new mobilisation plan entitled 'The Star' (*Zvezda*). Until then, a mobilisation plan 'Adriatic' (*Jadran*) remained valid.[9] Working on the new mobilisation plan 'The Star' started on 21 October 1949.[10]

According to the plan 'Pearl', the Yugoslav Army had in the most difficult period of the Cominform Crisis (1949–1950), five military districts with four armies, two mechanised corps, 21 rifle and four mountain divisions; 'Odred' was a 2000 strong Task Force in the Free Territory of Trieste, then the KNOJ with four divisions for interior duties and the border brigades, regiments and finally the Guards HQ with one Guards rifle division. There were 19 military territorial districts with 355 military territorial sections to manage

Spitfire Mk VC, serial 9486 (ex-RAF, BR 130) of the 103rd Reconnaissance Regiment seen here at Pančevo airfield in south Banat, after being transferred from Mostar to be much closer to the borders of the People Democracy countries. (Medija Centar Odbrana)

conscription and mobilisation. The Air Force had six air divisions, the Air Academy with two training regiments, four air technical divisions, three independent aviation regiments and a parachute battalion. The Yugoslav Navy had a fleet and four Naval Zones which controlled all of the shore units, which were not part of the fleet.

The 'wartime' organisation projected by this plan included the establishment of 'fronts' as the largest ground force HQs established by the military districts. They would become operational at the start of a general mobilisation. An additional four corps HQs, six rifle and six mountain divisions were planned to be mobilised. It was estimated that a peacetime structure of 360,000 men would grow to a million troops.[11]

Plan 'Pearl', already sanctioned, included movements of certain units at the turn of 1948–1949, according to the new strategic situation and the threat from the Soviets and its satellites. Several divisions were now transferred closer to the north, north-eastern and eastern parts of Yugoslavia, including the 16th from Kragujevac to Smederevska Palanka, the 36th from Banja Luka to Sremska Mitrovica, the 40th from Zrenjanin to Slavonska Požega, the 45th from Niš to Leskovac, the 50th from Ohrid to Kičevo and the 54th from Novo Mesto to Požarevac.[12] The movement of the schools and training units from border areas in Banat to deeper into Yugoslavia was also carried out in this period. For example, the Tank School moved from Bela Crkva to Banja Luka and the Signals School from Zrenjanin to Škofja Loka.[13]

In the Air Force, several important changes were implemented in the middle and second half of 1949. The 32nd Bomber Division (equipped with Pe-2 bombers) based at Sombor near the border with Hungary was moved to Zagreb-Pleso. Meanwhile, the 37th Strike Division (Il-2 Shturmoviks) moved from Zagreb-Pleso to Zagreb-Lucko airfield and to Cerklje. The Air Academy, which had its three training aviation regiments and other units in southern Banat was transferred to Mostar. From Mostar the Spitfire-equipped 103rd Recce Regiment moved to Pančevo closer to the area of eventual operations. To provide fighter defence for the Yugoslav capital, the 117th Fighter Regiment with Yak-9P fighters was transferred from Pula to Zemun/Belgrade airport. Construction work on a new air base with a concrete runway and better infrastructure, some 20 kilometres north of Belgrade between Batajnica and Nova Pazova villages, which had started in 1947, now became intensified.[14]

It seems that the plans outlined and carried out at the turn of 1949-1950, were not enough for Yugoslav senior commanders. A new reorganisation was ordered in June 1950, known as plan 'Flint' (*Kremen*).[15] This plan can be seen as a correction or adjustment to the previous plan and organisational scheme. Upon plan 'Flint', the Second Military District (Novi Sad) was turned into the 9th Corps and became part of the First Military District (Belgrade) which now became responsible for the territory of Vojvodina and the central parts of Serbia. The HQ of the Third Military District was moved from Niš to Skoplje. Four armies (VIII, IX, X and XII) were now

Adorned with pictures and slogans, this Dodge 3/4t Beep, leads a column of Dodge lorries carrying the infantry of the 6th Proletarian Rifle Division, during a parade held after an exercise, most likely in city of Karlovac, 1950. The iconography has changed, Tito and the members of the Yugoslav Central Committee are seen in the pictures. (Medija Centar Odbrana)

The 13th Proletarian Regiment marching somewhere near the border with Italy, 1952. (Medija Centar Odbrana)

Pupils of a high school during pre-military training, April 1951. (Author's Collection)

Fluctuation amongst the cadres was significant as there were thousands with different 'schooling' status, civilians and military personnel on temporary detachments, some of them in labour or construction units. The figures gathered by the Ministry of People's Defence, the General Staff and the Logistics Department frequently differed. Continuous reorganisations just confused the matter, despite orders issued in 1951 to establish a system to show the exact number of available men. The figures from 1951 showed that the number of servicemen in the Yugoslav Army was even higher than the previous year and that the discrepancies were still in the tens of thousands.

reduced to corps size (19th, 4th, 23rd and 11th). Two ambitious mechanised corps (IV and IX) were returned to tank division status (20th and 26th), while a third tank division (17th), was formed in the north-eastern part of Yugoslavia by the redistribution of existing tank brigades.

The introduction of the corps as the prime organisational form was the characteristic of this plan. Even in the Air Force, where in 1950 three aviation divisions were formed into the III Air Corps, the corps was now perceived as the main joint operational HQ which commanded and organised combat operations in one and eventually, two strategic directions, while logistical support was devolved to the HQ of the Military District.[16] In wartime, the formation of three 'fronts' ('G' in Belgrade, 'B' in Skoplje and 'C' in Zagreb) remained, to be implemented at the moment of aggression, along with a higher number of the new wartime infantry divisions which had to be formed.[17] The branch commands (Tank, Armoured, Air Defence, Chemical, et cetera) that existed at the level of the Ministry, now became departments.[18]

Looking at the order of battle of the 'Flint' plan, it becomes obvious that some of the units (divisions brigade and regiments) were renamed again, especially those which covered north-eastern areas of Yugoslavia, mostly from the former Second Military District. This may be a sign that some of the unit titles were compromised by defections or the intelligence services of the satellite armies. Other units were moved to new garrisons, some of them for the second or third time since the Crisis started. It could be concluded that the reorganisations of the Yugoslav Army were almost continuous and the various plans never fully implemented.

Another problem was estimating the exact number of servicemen within the army. Figures dated 15 March 1950, state that there were 357,492 men present out of 370,727 on paper.[19] The figures for 1 June 1951 were 394,272 present and 343,039 on paper. A significant number of 51,203 men (mostly conscripts) were supernumary. The number of surplus personnel grew through the year. At the end of 1951, there were 421,351 present, compared to the organisation strength which was 336,746 men. That meant there were 84,605 surplus personnel, again most of them being new conscripts. The number of surplus officers was between 2,300 to 3,400. Conversely, the figures showed a lack of NCOs and military servants.[20]

Adapting Military Schools to New Circumstances
The Cominform Crisis greatly influenced the system of Yugoslav military education. The possibility of educating or training personnel in the Soviet Union was removed and so the Yugoslav Army formed its own higher schools/academies. As soon as autumn of 1948, higher academies for the Ground Forces, Air Force, Navy and medical service were formed to provide leadership education for those branches. Nearly 50 ground forces generals went to the High Academy, as well as a number of the generals or admirals of the Air Force and Navy.[21]

Slowly, Soviet influence was replaced by the reintroduction of Yugoslav/Serbian Army terms and practices, along with some of the experiences of the Partisan movement. The term 'učilište' (college) taken from Soviet practice, was replaced by the term škola (school) or later akademija (academy) by the order of the Deputy MNO on 29 September 1950. In the same year, the Yugoslav Army had 44 different schools, including 21 for officers, 16 for NCOs and seven specialised schools.[22] From 1952–1953, many of them, belonging to the same branch, were joined into School Centres that almost became the home of active and reserve officers and NCOs of that certain branch; infantry at Sarajevo, armoured units at Banja Luka, aviation in Mostar, aviation-technical in Rajlovac, naval in Divulje and artillery and technical in Zagreb.[23]

Yugoslav military schools suffered from the same continuous changes in the period between 1949 and 1953 as other army units. Most of the generations of officers' that received their first ranks in this period, no matter the branch, kept only the number of the class (for example IV, V, or VI) during their education. The organisation and sometimes the location, could change several times during in this period. They could enrol in a 'učilište', continue their education through a 'school for active officers' and graduate from an 'academy' or 'school centre'. The year 1949 saw some of the biggest changes when several schools were transferred away from the borders. As some of the living conditions were not adequate upon their arrival, they continued their education in other neighbouring garrisons, or were helped to construct the new facilities.

Despite the problems, intensive education and training slowly improved the officers and NCO cadres within the Army. Most of the post-war cadres were, in many cases, former Partisans with little or no formal education. Several thousand officers graduated from the courses and academies in the Soviet Union in the period 1944–1948 but only within the Air Force did Soviet educated officers outnumber Yugoslav educated ones.

Educated Officers in Yugoslavia and the Soviet Union 1944–1948[24]		
Educated in:	**FNR Yugoslavia**	**Soviet Union**
Infantry	8,276	914
Cavalry	54	40
Artillery	1,988	310
Anti-aircraft Artillery	746	53
Artillery Technical Branch	435	137
Armoured Units	1,139	256
Engineers	1,138	168
Air Force	874	1,166
Navy	1,089	134
Chemical Protection	420	54
Technical Service	502	42
Geodetic Service	404	7
Military Economy Service	1,640	39
Medical Service	560	112
Veterinarian Service	60	29

Another important factor was that most of cadets enrolled in military schools as youngsters without any knowledge or interest in politics. However, at the graduation ceremony some three or four years later, nearly all of them were members of the Communist Party of Yugoslavia.

In April 1954, the Central Committee of the Communist Party discussed applications to military academies and schools in the previous two years. Among other facts and figures, they noted concern about several trends or problems in the recruitment of new officer cadres. These included the fewer youngsters interested in becoming officers so half of the places remained unfulfilled. It was especially clear that in the largest cities (Belgrade, Ljubljana and Zagreb), those who finished gymnasiums (high schools) or had higher grades, were the least interested in being officers. Later in 1958, it was concluded that over 80 percent of cadets came from the peasantry.[25] Finally, there were also national variations, as most cadets were Serbs or Montenegrins. The Central Committee concluded that Slovenes and Croats were significantly less likely to apply than Serbs and Montenegrins'.[26]

A key ideological basis for both morale and recruitment in the Yugoslav Army came to be so-called 'socialist patriotism'.[27] The break between Tito and Stalin, produced the idea among military-political theorists in the Army to create and to strengthen a 'higher type of patriotism', under the leadership of the Communist Party and on the principle of 'proletarian internationalism'. Such socialist patriotism was explained as combination between the 'love of country and the love of socialism', which was the 'most important feature of our new patriotism'.[28] The period after 1948 brought the establishment of a new Yugoslav myth, based on the idea that Tito's Partisan forces fought their own fight during the Second World War. This myth included the notion of a general Yugoslav character and the fight for the restoration of a unified Yugoslavia, on the basis of

Cadets of the Infantry Officers School (known with the abbreviation 'Posh') seen here during an exercise in 1950. The cadets are wearing Italian M-33 steel combat helmets, mostly used at that time in the 7th Military District (HQ Sarajevo). They prepare obsolete but still useful, former 75mm Gebrigskannone 15. (Medija Centar Odbrana)

The training ship *Jadran* was used from 1949 for training Naval Academy cadets. The *Jadran* had served the same purpose in the Navy of the Kingdom of Yugoslavia. (Medija Centar Odbrana)

equality in both the national and the social sense. The Cominform Crisis increased the Yugoslav people's trust in the Army and even their identification with it.

Towards the end of 1951, standardised Yugoslav war flags with standard Yugoslav colours were introduced for regiments and brigades. The Air Force had a specific blue colour but with elements of Yugoslav symbols. The only exceptions were the elite units of the

Army; the guard units and the proletarian units that kept the red flags with ideological symbols. In the spirit of equality of alphabets, the words embroidered on the flags, 'For the freedom and honour of the socialist homeland' or the unit's name, were on the left side in the Latin alphabet and on the right in Cyrillic. These flags were presented to regiments and brigades by Marshal Tito himself at special celebrations in the period from December 1951 to September 1954. In the later phases, there were exceptions to the rule and the flags were presented by delegates of the Supreme Commander.[29]

Technical Problems Influence Combat Readiness

The sudden break in military relations with the Soviet Union occurred during the reorganisation of the Yugoslav Army and planned development based on deliveries of armaments and equipment from the Soviet Union, or from Czechoslovakia or Poland. The cessation of these deliveries caused a lot of problems for the Yugoslav Army, especially in important branches such as armoured units, the artillery and the Air Force. Tito, did not exaggerate when he addressed the Party members of the First Proletarian Division on 14 July 1948, saying, 'The situation today is, comrades, very difficult'.[30]

To overcome the problems of available equipment and armaments, during the spring of 1949, several councils were created for planning the development and equipment of all army branches, first at the level of the Ministry and then later, at that of the General Staff. Those councils had to plan the development of their branches in the context of the difficulties of the Cominform Crisis.[31]

The main problem for the Yugoslav armoured units was maintaining the required level of combat readiness, which was severely hampered by the lack of spare parts and fuel. In the artillery, the biggest problems were the lack of towing vehicles, insufficient larger calibre howitzers and guns compared to possible aggressors and inadequate accommodation in several of the garrisons of the Fifth Military District.[32] A lack of vehicles in the Army was also noted by Tito in his interview to *The New York Times*, in November 1950. Tito said 'The situation with lorries was very weak. Lorries that we received

through UNRRA arrived without spare parts and those parts are badly needed by us'.[33]

The Yugoslav Navy received Italian vessels as part of reparations for Royal Yugoslav Navy ships captured or destroyed in the war. They arrived between September 1948 and January 1949; seven minesweepers, four escort destroyers, four tugboats, four fuel tankers and three motor gunboats.[34] But the Navy lacked torpedoes, because their repair and production was still not restored, as well as mines and heavier calibre guns on all available combat ships.[35]

General Ulepič, who commanded the Yugoslav Air Force from 1946, estimated that following the start of the Crisis there was a very complex situation. Existing equipment was exhausted, the level of airworthiness was lower than normal (except for the new Yak-9P fighters), the halting of deliveries hampered the development of new

The Central Tank Workshop in Mladenovac, a town some 56 kilometres south of Belgrade, was the main hub for overhauling all armoured vehicles in the Yugoslav Army. It continued to operate in the former Wehrmacht Herman Goering Werke, established in 1941. Here, a freshly overhauled T-34 tank is seen during testing in 1948. (Medija Centar Odbrana)

Very basic conditions for repairing an aircraft at Zagreb air base in 1951. A Yakovlev UT-2 trainer is being overhauled. (Medija Centar Odbrana)

Looking very motley, with a variety of equipment and by their general appearance, soldiers of an artillery unit are seen at a parade, after the Sumadija manoeuvres of 1949. They wore a variety of German, Czech and shortened-German helmets, On the other hand, the infantry unit appears to be a much smarter outfit. (Medija Centar Odbrana)

It was standard practice during the Cominform Crisis that all vital and scarce aircraft and vehicle parts should be additionally protected and cared for. Here, the engine cowlings and cockpits of Soviet LI-2 transports are covered with linen to protect them from the sun. In front of the aircraft, a guard is armed with an Italian M-1891 Carcano rifle. (Medija Centar Odbrana)

units and combat aircraft had to be converted into trainers to enable cadets to finish their training.[36] Lists of aviation unit strengths show that were 738 airworthy aircraft in December 1949 and 703 a year later. The number of grounded aircraft that remained in the units was 80 in December 1949 and 113 in December 1950. Most of them were combat aircraft. The HQ of the Air Force tried to overcome the problem by gathering units with the same or similar types of aircraft at one air base. A 'temporary downgrading' was especially seen within fighter aviation. The lack of advanced trainers in 1950, made General Ulepič ask Deputy Minister General Gošnjak to determine more realistic targets for the development of the Air Force, as previous experience showed the current plans were unfeasible. Without safe and secured finances, the number of pilots which had to be trained could not be estimated.[37]

In general, logistics were heavily overburdened. Every day, three-daily meals for 280,000 and partial rations for another 370,000 personnel had to be catered for. Due to a shortage of cattle, one or

two days per week were proclaimed as 'meatless'. An unexpected drought during the whole of 1951 and part of 1952 produced more difficulties in feeding the army. Some HQs were given the authority to organise the feeding of their men using their own resources.[38]

An important test for the combat readiness of the Yugoslav Army during the earlier part of the crisis were large manoeuvres organised in the second part of September 1949, in an area some 60 to 80 kilometres south of Belgrade, near Sumadija. This first largest exercise after the Second World War was known as the 'Sumadija manoeuvres'. Over 20,000 men were engaged from the Ground

Yugoslav military leadership with Marshal Tito at the main stage during the parade after the Sumadija manoeuvres, September 1949. Of note is the iconography with pictures of the Yugoslav Communist Party Central Committee members. (Medija Centar Odbrana)

Two dozen paratroopers of the 46th Air Landing Battalion, packed in the rear of a GMC adorned with slogans, seen at a military parade after the Sumadija manoeuvres. It was the first near-to-combat debut for Yugoslav paratroopers. (Medija Centar Odbrana)

Carrying white 'aggressor' stripes, this YAK-3 fighter, serial 2254/54, belonging to the 116th Fighter Regiment, is being loosely camouflaged by its groundcrew during the Sumadija manoeuvres at Knić airfield. (Medija Centar Odbrana)

Interesting image of a Yugoslav Navy landing fleet during a large exercise that included the simulation of an amphibious landing on the Adriatic coast, mid-1951. Among other vessels here are former Italian Navy RD minesweepers M301 and M302 and two auxiliary ships (PB-21, the former Royal Yugoslav *Sitnica* and PT-11, formerly Dutch and then Kreigesmarine) with other smaller vessels. (Medija Centar Odbrana)

and Air Forces, including paratroopers. The exercise was commanded by the Deputy Chief of the General Staff, General Peko Dapčević. The overall scenario was 'breaking through an organised defence with the assistance of an air landing'. The main combat between the Red and Blue sides lasted for two days. The Blues organised a defensive system of trenches and fortifications. The Reds had to break through the Blue lines, with a tank assault to join up with paratroopers dropped in the Blue's rear. The prevailing concept was an attack in which the tank units had an important role.[39] The atmosphere during the manoeuvres was characterised by a wartime spirit. The history of the 116th Fighter Regiment noted that observers commented on a war-like level of commitment and 'not the false impression of some peacetime exercise'.[40]

After the manoeuvres and dispersal of the troops, on 1 October 1949, Tito gave a very aggressive speech against the Soviets and their satellites. Around him on the stage, were military and 'political' generals – prominent members of the Central Committee.[41] At the lunch reserved only for high-ranking officers and commanders of the units engaged in manoeuvres, Tito was much more serious, allegedly saying to the gathered generals and colonels:

Maybe I shall not live to see the victory of truth. Maybe Bevc [Edvard Kardelj] or Koča [General Popović] and their generation will not either. But I am convinced that someone from your generation will, my young comrades. Even if a high price needs to be paid to defend freedom with arms. Comrades, if we do not live long enough to see this, I am giving You the task: do not let anything distract you, keep on fighting and do not mourn the victims.[42]

The Building of an Indigenous Military Industry

The building or rebuilding of Yugoslav military industrial capacity after 1948 was urgently needed after the expected reliance on the Soviet military ended abruptly and was another of the consequences of the Crisis. For previous delays in its development, Tito and the contemporary press blamed the Soviets, explaining that they had suggested to the Yugoslavs not to bother developing their local military industry but to rely on Soviet supplies instead. Commenting on the finances needed for an armaments industry, Tito explained in parliament at the end of 1950:

Almost 100,000 German POWs remained in Yugoslavia after the war, many until 1951. They were organised into working battalions and were used for various kinds of military and civil infrastructure projects. Here, seen at Belgrade docks in 1946. (Medija Centar Odbrana)

…we were still fooled by the illusions that we can rely on the Soviet Union for everything, that we do not need our own factories for producing different types of armament for our Army. We believed their words that they would provide us brotherly help, that they would give us the required weapons …'

This led, Tito said, to the situation that an armaments industry 'did not enter into' the five-year industrial development plan that was outlined in 1947.[43]

The first five-year plan for the development of industry (the so-called *petoletka*) was approved on the eve of conflict with the Soviets, in March 1948. This plan projected the building of 15 new military factories, the rebuilding of two which were damaged in the war and the establishment of military production sections in nine other factories. It was hoped that the plan would be fulfilled by the end of 1952.[44] It was a bold decision, given that the technological level of the armaments industry in Yugoslavia was very low with obsolete or inadequate equipment and tools. Almost everything was lacking; skilled personnel, materials, spare parts for machines, technical documentation and even electrical power. In some cases, production techniques had not progressed from traditional artisan workshops.

During this period, some machinery and tools were received from Germany as war reparations. The planned purchases of complete factories from Poland and Czechoslovakia were abandoned. To remedy the shortage of skilled labour, soldiers with the necessary technical knowledge were transferred to industry. German POWs were also used in many factories in 1948 and 1949. After an analysis of the new strategic situation, the construction of five factories was cancelled, three planned factories were moved and the decision was taken to build five more factories (signals equipment, infantry weaponry, ammunition and demolition devices) and to overhaul several workshops.[45]

Following the emerging threat from the East, some important factories were to be built in areas out of reach of imminent danger from aggression. These projects faced large obstacles, as many of the remote towns and villages in Bosnia and Herzegovina had no

Local production of Higgins torpedo boats known as series TC-108, based on the examples that were used by Yugoslav Navy from 1945, was established at the small Ivan Cetinić shipyard on Korčula island. (Medija Centar Odbrana)

previous industrial developments and inadequate road and rail links to enable rapid construction. In other cases, a number of already existing military factories were transferred from areas 'exposed to eventual aggression' (many around Belgrade or central Serbia) to distant areas in Bosnia-Herzegovina or parts of Slovenia. In the urgency of the Crisis, there were not many discussions about it. But in the period prior to the dissolution of Yugoslavia in the 1990s, there was much public debate in Serbia about the transfer of industry out of the republic nearly half a century previously.

The constructions of new factories or other military infrastructure was under the firm scrutiny of KOS and UDBA officers. There was concern, almost fear, that a large number of workers or soldiers would disrupt the new factory or construction site. It was noted that this had already happened during the building of the Tito military factory near Sarajevo.[46]

In the case of the Navy, some advantage was gained by the annexation of the Istra and Kvarner areas, in which large shipyards existed, notably in Pula (Pola), Mali Lošinj (Lossinpiccolo) and Rijeka (Reka, Fiume). Important assets, such as the previous Ganz-Danubius or Lazareus shipyards were mostly found to be damaged or emptied of machinery and tools. After 1948, the rebuilding of such shipyards began and they were soon capable of carrying out repairs on existing vessels of the fleet. As the Cominform Crisis continued they were able to build original or copied vessels in small or even large series. The shipyards were under the control of the Ministry of People's Defence and remained so until 1953.[47]

At the level of the Ministry of People's Defence, several Central Departments for military industries, shipyards and military construction projects were established in 1949. The number of personnel employed in the military industry was around 30,000 during the crisis, reaching a peak in 1950–1951 with some 50,000 engaged or employed as personnel. At many of the sites where new factories were being built, the number of construction workers ranged between 1,000 and 5,000 per site, mostly made up of conscript soldiers and POWs. The General Directorate for military construction works controlled around 22 military construction enterprises with some 55,000 workers or attached troops, operating at numerous sites in the period between 1948 and 1954.[48] General Gosnjak explained in his report to the members of the People's Parliament, that a total of 37 military factories had been built so far, 'Among them 36 are working' he explained.[49] It was a success, despite the quality of the products.

Types of Armaments Produced

The products that were produced in the emerging Yugoslav armaments industry were of various kinds and origins. There were pre-war projects, a few new projects and in many cases the weaponry was simply copied from German, or to a lesser extent Soviet, models. As a kind of leading body in military design and testing, a Military-Technical Institute was created in the Belgrade suburbs in 1949. It was engaged in several projects that were finalised in this period, including the B-1 mountain gun, M-48A rifle, RB anti-tank launcher and others.

Despite the level of wartime destruction, the *Crvena zastava* (Red Star) factory started production of a series of M-48 (Gewehr 98 or pre-war Yugoslav M-1924) 7.92 rifles, M-49 7.62 submachine guns (PPSh 41 Špagin) and later M-53 machineguns (MG-42). The *Krušik* factory at Valjevo continued its pre-war production of hand grenades, starting with the M-47, then the M-50 and then, the standard Yugoslav Army hand grenade, the M-52. The same factory started production of the M-49 grenade launcher. By simply copying Soviet mines, three types were produced at the Tito Factory and Main Engineer Workshop; the PMD, PMR-1 and anti-tank TMD-1.[50] Various types of ammunition and grenades were produced in eight different factories in Valjevo, Vogošća, Sarajevo, Titovo Užice, Konjic, Gorazde, Čačak and Bugojno.[51]

Production of artillery pieces met with many more difficulties than smaller armaments and equipment. There were many projects and prototypes which did not enter service, including a recoilless 82mm gun (developed and tested between 1949 and 1951) and a 85mm anti-tank gun in 1950. The *Crvena zastava* factory had simply copied the French Brandt Mle 31 82mm mortar to produce them in the period 1948–1951. VTI developed and produced an indigenous 120mm mortar UB (M-52) between 1949 and 1952. The most successful artillery piece that was produced in this period was the B-1 76mm mountain gun, later known as the M-48. The first

The Soviet PPsh 41 Špagin submachinegun was produced in Yugoslavia without licence as the Automat M-49 calibre 7.62 in *Crvena Zastava* plants (Enterprise No.44) in Kragujevac. (Medija Centar Odbrana)

The production line of the M-53 (German MG-42) 7.92 machinegun, also produced in *Crvena Zastava* plants. (Medija Centar Odbrana)

series (12 pieces) was produced in the *Crvena zastava* factory and from 1950 production shifted to the newly built *Bratstvo* factory, which made a batch of 62 by the end of 1950. Later produced in large quantities, the M-48 also became an important Yugoslav export product.[52]

A very peculiar episode of Yugoslav military production during the Cominform Crisis, was a tank named *Vozilo A* (Vehicle A). The construction and production of the tank was mostly organised in the Central Tank Workshop in Mladenovac, which already carried out repair and overhauls on all of the armoured vehicles

The Yugoslav 76mm B-1 mountain gun, later widely known as the M-48, seen here during initial trials during 1948/1949. (Medija Centar Odbrana)

The M-48 76mm series gun, seen here during final painting, prior to delivery to the units. Besides the Yugoslav Army it served in many other armies all over the world and became known as the 'Tito Gun'. (Medija Centar Odbrana)

in Yugoslav Army service and even produced some smaller parts for the Soviet T-34 tank and SU-76 self-propelled gun. One of the T-34s was simply disassembled and the copying of the parts began. Some of the components were changed, most significantly the turret. The Yugoslavs added an AA machine gun and made some other improvements or variations depending on their available tools and technology. Despite a generally similar appearance, each of the five tanks was different in many details. It was concluded that every vehicle was 'tested separately, which then hindered serious conclusions'.[53]

Actually, the appearance of the five Yugoslav-built tanks at the May Day parade in 1950 on Belgrade's streets, gave a significant morale boost not just for the members of the Army and Party but also for the broader public in Yugoslavia. It was announced that Yugoslav industry could produce the tanks in a short period of time and that pressure from the East did not limit the capabilities nor the morale of Yugoslav workers.[54] In reality, in August 1951, the General Staff decided that *Vozilo A* prototypes were not satisfactory, as they were built in 'craft' conditions, with various production procedures and without proper technical documentation.[55]

In the May Day parade of 1950, besides the five indigenous tanks, a series of *Pionir* lorries appeared. This was a Yugoslav production of the Czech Praga RW 2.5t lorry. This type was produced in a factory in Rakovica and then production moved to TAM in Maribor. It was also proudly displayed at contemporary parades and fairs. In fact, it was a weak and already obsolete vehicle for military service. In the same period, the Rakovica factory and TAM produced prototypes of another lorry named *Prvenac* (the first one) and two tractors *Udarnik* (Striker Worker) and *Zadrugar*. (Member of Cooperative). TAM and many other military workshops also overhauled and produced spare parts for GMC lorries. Some conversions of the standard lorries to fuel tanks were also carried out.[56]

All five *Vozilo A* Yugoslav-built tanks seen here prior to the May Day military parade in 1950, lined-up at Banjica Field in the Belgrade suburbs. All five of them wore different slogans. After the parade, they were mostly used for displays and later for training. No further production continued. It was a huge and expensive setback for the modest Yugoslav industries. (Medija Centar Odbrana)

Yugoslav infantry with Czech helmets, mounted on Praga RN lorries, during a military parade in Belgrade 1949. This type was produced under licence in a factory in the Belgrade suburb of Rakovica, between 1947–1950 and the TAM factory in Maribor, between 1947 and 1959. It became an important addition to the modest Yugoslav Army vehicle fleet during the Cominform Crisis. (Medija Centar Odbrana)

In the period between 1945 and 1951, Yugoslav military industries produced 144,876 7.92mm rifles, 216 mountain 76mm guns, 10,294 grenade launchers with over 100,000 grenades, 264 million 7.92 bullets, some 1.5 billion 82mm and 120mm mortar rounds, 479,000 hand grenades, 286,000 different mines and the prototype five tanks. Overcoming structural and production problems, such quantities did much to strengthen the ground forces of the Yugoslav Army.

The interruption of military relations with the Soviets and satellites had a serious impact on the nascent Yugoslav aviation industry, as well the development of the Yugoslav Air Force. The Air Force lacked the continuous flow of new types which should have replaced the wartime airframes. Some of the projects relied on engines and equipment from Czechoslovakia.[57] Production of the Aero-2 light basic trainer started in 1948 and continued during the Crisis, reaching over 280 produced examples in several different versions. The introduction of Aero-2 into the units enabled the continuation of basic training for new pilots. It was also used in the combat units so that the pilots could maintain flying skills while minimising the hours of the combat types.[58]

The first couple of Swiss Saurer 4GE-L trucks in Yugoslavia, seen during trials in the winter of 1952. This type was widely produced later as the 'FAP', coming from *Fabrika Automobila Priboj*. The FAP was produced for decades in different versions for the Yugoslav Army and civil market. (Medija Centar Odbrana)

Marshal Tito, with the senior commanders of the Yugoslav Army and Air Force, seen here inspecting the first prototype of the Ikarus S-49A piston-engined fighter, at Zemun/Belgrade airport, 21 May 1950. (Medija Centar Odbrana)

Colonel Beslin's almost strange-looking group of projects produced in the Ikarus factory, 1950–1952 seen at Batajnica air base. From left to right: 452 and 451M jets; and 451 and 232 with the pilot in a prone position. (Authors Collection)

The first batch of Ikarus S-49C piston-engined fighters, improved with the Hispano Suiza 12 Z-17 engine, seen here in early 1952, after being rolled out of the Ikarus factory, at Zemun/Belgrade Airport. (Medija Centar Odbrana)

A few prototypes were tested in this early stage of Crisis but they did not enter production, for example the Ikarus 211, 231, 251 and 252 May Day. Also tested were the 232 *Pionir* and 451 in which the pilot was in a prone position. Two twin-engined types built at Ikarus were tested in 1949: the 214 which crashed on its maiden flight but later entered a small series production and the 215, which never entered serial production.[59]

Arguably, the most successful type produced during the crisis was Ikarus S-49 piston-engined fighter. This type was built using the pre-war construction plans for the *Rogozarski* IK-3 fighter which was produced in small series prior to the Axis invasion of Yugoslavia in April 1941. Instead of a Hispano Suiza engine, the S-49 was fitted with a Soviet VK-105 engine, giving it more of a Yak appearance than the IK-3 had. This type was tested in 1949 and a series of 45 examples was completed during 1950. This version entered service with the Belgrade-based 44th Fighter Division.[60] Yugoslavia siding with NATO, enabled further development of this type by replacing the VK engine with the French Hispano Suiza. This version, the S-49C, was produced in a large series in the 1952–1953 period and

A total of 72 'Higgins' torpedo boats were produced, many of them exported to Third World navies. Here, TC-118 with an Admiral's pennant is seen during one of the naval exercises in 1951. (Medija Centar Odbrana)

The first series of Yugoslav indigenous patrol boats, PBR-501 or Kraljevica Class, were built from 1951. They entered the service within the 38th Patrol Boat Squadron. (Author's Collection)

used mostly in training and second-line units. Despite the type being obsolete compared to jet fighters in other Air Forces, the S-49 gave YAF pilots and personnel a significant morale boost and was later used as a transition aircraft between Soviet piston-engined Yaks and American jets.[61]

Besides the efforts to build a fleet of various indigenous types, the Ikarus factory produced its first jet aeroplane, the 451M. It was constructed by Lieutenant Colonel Bešlin, who became famous for constructing several advanced and concept types. His 451M was powered by two under-wing Turbomeca Pallas 056A jet engines and had its maiden flight on 25 October 1952. During 1952–1953, Bešlin worked on another jet fighter, the 452M, with the same engines but positioned in the fuselage. It had its maiden flight on 24 July 1953 but crashed soon after.[62] These types, as well as a few others that Beslin constructed later in the mid-1950s, can be regarded only as experimental and as the result of enormous Yugoslav efforts to possess the jet fighters as soon as possible. It is worth noting that Yugoslav military negotiators insisted in their talks in France, Switzerland and later in Great Britain and the United States between 1949 and 1951, on deliveries of jets and even licenced production for its Air Force. The desire to possess jet aircraft was enormous and it may have been the case that Yugoslav irritated their hosts by insisting on them in a period when such types were still in the development phase, with many unsolved construction or production problems.

The Cominform Crisis led to the development of a shipbuilding programme called the First Fleet Programme, organised in shipyards in Pula, Reka, Kraljevica, Mali Lošinj, Trogir, Split, Korčula and Vela Luka. During the course of the Cominform Crisis, the Yugoslav Navy received several new types of vessels. In the first phase of the Crisis, the most significant were the mine-sweeper classes ML-101 and TČ-108 and a large series of Higgins torpedo boats based on the PT-201 type. These were followed by a series of auxiliary ships. From 1951, a series of landing/minelaying ships, DTM-213, were produced in Split and a series of 24 PBR-501 patrol boats were produced in Kraljevica, most of them exported to Third World navies.[63]

Some vessels were recovered from the sea, repaired and put into active service. This was the case with a former Italian submarine which was named 802 *Sava*.[64] The Italian cargo ship *Ramb III* was

also raised from the sea, repaired and became the training ship *Galeb*, which was later used mostly by Marshall Tito in his 'paths to peace' visits to Africa and Asia, as well by the cadets of the Naval Academy in their training cruises around the Mediterranean.[65]

The revised First Fleet Programme was indeed a huge effort to strengthen the Yugoslav Navy. Together with ships obtained from Italy as reparations and vessels recovered from the sea, the number of vessels produced in several shipyards along the Adriatic Coast was significant.

First Fleet Programme – Revised 1948–1952[66]		
Type Of Vessel	**Planned**	**Entered Service**
Escort Destroyers	4	4
Patrol Boats	8	8
Submarines	1	1
Torpedo Boats	56	55
Minelayers	4	12
Minesweepers	16	17
Landing Ships	48	35
School Ships	2	2
Auxiliary Ships	78	75
River Vessels	51	33
TOTAL	268	242

Despite the significant increase in ship numbers, the Yugoslav naval senior commanders were not satisfied. They did not fear the Soviet Navy, since it was far from Adriatic but they compared the Yugoslav Navy with the Italian Navy throughout the whole period, which had six-times more ship tonnage. Tito himself concluded in July 1951, 'our Navy was still small. It is not the most modern. Our vessels are almost obsolete ...' But he promised that the budget for the Navy would be, year by year, raised 'to the Navy's needs'.[67]

7
TO THE END OF THE CRISIS

Yugoslavia Sides with West

After the first suspicions of conflict in the communist camp, the Allies started to realise that it could be useful to support Yugoslavia. First of all, in increasing its military capabilities.[1] The planners at the US State Department had been swift to exploit the opportunity to sow maximum discord in the communist bloc in Europe. US officials remarked that Yugoslavia was of direct importance to the security of the United States and it was decided that military and economic aid should be given to Yugoslavia so that its ability to face the Soviet threat was enhanced.[2]

Negotiations between Yugoslav and US Army officials took place throughout 1951. The Yugoslavs strongly insisted on their urgent needs, while the Americans focused on their capabilities and strategic intentions. Key meetings for the delivery of military aid were held during Colonel General Koča Popović's two visits to the United States. However, even during the negotiations, some weapon deliveries were sent to the Yugoslavs, to fulfil some of their immediate requirements.[3] These pre-deliveries included some light piston-engined aeroplanes, artillery pieces, vehicles and other urgently needed items.

US officials claimed that the war in Korea caused a shortage of some of the armaments and equipment that the Yugoslavs needed. Also, the Yugoslavs tried to convince the Americans that they were interested only in up-to-date equipment because they did not plan to lead a Partisan-type campaign if the Soviets invaded. Following the Second World War, there was a deeply held view in some other nations that while the Yugoslav Army may have been a strong Partisan movement, it lacked a modern technological culture. Among the US Army officials, there was an intention to deploy military advisors to Yugoslavia along with the equipment.[4]

Prior to the signing of the Mutual Assistance Pact, several military exercises were performed for the Chief of Staff of the US Army, General J. Lawton Collins, who visited Yugoslavia. The aim of his visit was to gather information about the Yugoslav Army's quality and potential. The largest exercise took part in the Banja Luka area where armoured, airborne and aviation units were engaged in an assault over the Vrbas River. Yugoslavs claimed that this exercise impressed the US Army officials, which led to the cancelling of plans to send advisors in large numbers.[5]

The Military Assistance Pact was finally signed between the officials of the Yugoslav and the US government in Belgrade on 14 November 1951. According to this Pact, Yugoslavia was introduced into the framework of the Mutual Defence Aid Programme (MDAP). Yugoslav orders for equipment would be fulfilled by the United

Some of the weaponry was delivered even before the signing of the MDAP on 14 November 1951, including US M-1 75mm pack howitzers, as seen here during 1951. (Medija Centar Odbrana)

Colonel Nikola Lekic, who led the first group of Yugoslav airmen to be trained by the USAF on the F-47D Thunderbolt, greets the USAF representatives after landing at Shaw AFB. (Ladislav Žanović Family)

NATO military representatives at the military Mayday parade, 1951 in Belgrade. (Medija Centar Odbrana)

NATO and AMAS officers seen here during an inspection of a Military Academy exercise, near Topola, 1952. (Medija Centar Odbrana)

Lieutenant General Maxwell D. Taylor, US Army Deputy Chief of Staff for Operations and a notable commander of the US 101st Airborne Division during the Allied landing in Normandy, who accompanied the Assistant Secretary of Defence Frank C. Nash, during his visit to Yugoslavia in mid-August 1952. Taylor is seen here, holding a Yugoslav M-48 Mauser rifle during an inspection of Belgrade garrison units at Banjica Field. (Medija Centar Odbrana)

States, Great Britain and France. The Presidium of the Yugoslav Parliament ratified the Pact on 9 January 1952. It described this act as resistance to the Soviet military threat and blockade and that it was rooted in the principles of the United Nations.[6]

In an interview which coincided with the signing of the MAP, Marshal Tito stressed 'that military purchases from the United States do not mean a change to our independent policy and specific development of socialism; we want the United States to supply us with items that we do not possess'. Tito added that the strengthening of Yugoslav military capabilities would contribute to greater stability and peace in south-eastern Europe.[7] Equipment deliveries within the framework of the MDAP enabled qualitative and quantitative growth for the *Jugoslovenska Narodna Armija* (JNA, The Yugoslav People's Army. The term 'People's' was introduced on 22 December 1951[8]).

By the first weeks of 1952, military assistance agreed upon as part of the MDAP, began to be delivered to Yugoslavia, by ships or by air, in the case of the Air Force. In the same period, the groups of Yugoslav Army personnel received training on various types of armaments in the United States, Great Britain or at different US and NATO bases in Europe.

Yugoslav Army Joins the Mutual Defence Aid Programme

During Yugoslav's inclusion in the MDAP scheme, which lasted until the beginning of 1958, the Yugoslav Army received large batches of armaments and equipment.[9] Yugoslav-NATO cooperation in the 1950s requires its own specialised study. Some equipment, weaponry and other items were received successfully during 1951, prior to Yugoslavia formally joining the MDAP programme. All the beans used by the Yugoslav Army to feed its troops between 1951 and 1954 came from US assistance. There were also shipments of wheat, French beans, lard, sugar and oats for cattle.[10] During 1951, the Yugoslav Army also received quantities of 105mm howitzers, 57mm anti-tank guns, armoured vehicles, various artillery and infantry munitions, quantities of captured German infantry weapons and 10 former RAF liaison aircraft.[11]

Yugoslav ground forces received large quantities of weaponry. Those included over 5,000 60mmm and 88.9mm Bazookas, 1,120 recoilless guns of calibre 57mm and 75mm, 2,500 Browning M2.5 machineguns and 34,000 M-1 Thompson.45 submachineguns. Yugoslav armoured units were in a 'stormy period influenced by the sudden flow of the new fighting and non-fighting vehicles' delivered through the MDAP system. The equipment received included 599 M4A3 calibre 76mm Sherman tanks and 319 M-47 Patton tanks, 715 M-7 Priest, M-18 Hellcat and M-36 Jackson self-propelled guns and 565 M3A1 scout cars and M8 Greyhound armoured cars.

Immediately after the MAP was signed, a huge amount of artillery started to reach Yugoslavia. A total of 760 weapons of

Marshal Tito accompanied by the Commander of the US 6th Fleet Vice Admiral John H. Cassady and Yugoslav Navy senior officers, on the deck of the USS *Coral Sea*, Adriatic Sea, September 1952. (Muzej Jugoslavije)

105mm, 155mm and 203mm calibres were delivered. The scale of the received MDAP artillery equipment allowed for unit changes. The Yugoslavs decided to rearm the artillery within their eight divisions and to establish large numbers of independent anti-tank or howitzer artillery regiments, especially on the Corps, Army and Supreme Command Reserve levels. Besides guns, the Yugoslav artillery received ammunition, towing tractors and communication equipment. The MDAP equipment solved an acute Yugoslav shortage of towing vehicles. American M-4 and M-5 tractors were introduced for towing artillery pieces of 105–203mm calibres. For smaller calibres, mostly GMC lorries were used.

Another important type to be delivered to Yugoslavia was the Republic F-47D Thunderbolt. A total of 150 were delivered from 1951 to 1953. Seen here are Thunderbolts of the 111st Aviation Regiment, Cerklje 1953. (Medija Centar Odbrana)

Seen here in early 1952 are de Havilland Mosquito NF38s of the 103rd Reconnaissance Regiment at Pancevo airfield. Overpainted RAF roundels and serials are clearly visible. (Medija Centar Odbrana)

Some of the types of armaments received through the MDAP from 1951:

M-8 Greyhound armoured car of the 4th Guards Division, Belgrade, winter 1952/53.

A 'Long Tom' or M-1 155mm gun, May Day military parade, Belgrade 1954.

M4A3 Sherman, seen after the manoeuvres at Zagorje, late September 1953.

Dodge WC-54 ambulance, seen at the May Day military parade, Belgrade 1955.

M3A1 Scout Car leading a column of the M-18 Hellcat gun motor carriages during manoeuvres at Zagorje, September 1953.

One of the first batches of M-47 tanks, seen here being off-loaded from a ship, Reka harbour mid-1953. (Medija Centar Odbrana)

M-1 155mm howitzer, seen during the winter of 1955.

Anti-aircraft artillery was strengthened with nearly 1,000 artillery pieces of 40mm, 90mm and 94mm calibre. Radars for AA artillery guidance were also introduced. These deliveries enabled the Yugoslavs to form several 'heavy' anti-aircraft regiments armed with 90–94mm guns, which could handle targets up to 6,000 metres altitude and at night as well. The 40mm guns were introduced into infantry divisions for their AA defence. Yugoslav Army engineers received 44 different items covering 119 different types of equipment, including bridges, bulldozers, graders, rollers, boats and workshops. Yugoslav requests for modern equipment were partly fulfilled. Deliveries included 4,387 radios, 545 generators, 30 teleprinters and 24 workshop-vans. All these deliveries influenced the Yugoslavs to adopt many US Army standards and procedures.

The Yugoslav Air Force started to receive aircraft before the MDAP. Amongst the first were 140 piston-engined de Havilland Mosquitos.[12] These reached Yugoslavian skies from late October 1951 onwards. By the beginning of 1952, deliveries of the Republic F-47D Thunderbolt fighter bombers had begun. The Yugoslavs, which had an Air Force on the edge of collapse, welcomed these new 'birds' with praise. Marshal Tito showed enormous interest in MDAP deliveries and he was especially interested in the Air Force. In the middle of January 1952, he visited Pula air base to inspect just delivered F-47Ds. Tito remarked in front of

Yugoslav pilots obtained first-hand experience on jet fighters in the USAF 48th Fighter-Bomber Wing at Chaumont Air Base, France, in two courses held from September to March 1953. Here, Lieutenant Nikola Maravić poses with one of the US pilots near a F-84G Thunderjet. (Nikola Maravić Family)

A symbolic photo of Tito's Yugoslavia siding with NATO; a Yugoslav Air Force guardsman stands in front of a Lockheed T-33A, after the ceremony for the delivery of the first jets to Yugoslavia, 10 March 1953. This particular aircraft was serial USAF 51-8727 and JRV 10002 and served successfully until the mid-1970s in numerous Yugoslav aviation units. (Medija Centar Odbrana)

the airmen that he was more than satisfied with the new aircraft. A key moment in YAF development as part of the framework of the MDAP, was the introduction of jet aviation. The first batch of Lockheed T-33A trainers reached Batajnica air base on 10 March 1953. Other batches of 25 T-33A trainers and 167 Republic F-84G Thunder jets were delivered between 1953 and 1957. The number of transport aircraft was doubled with 20 Douglas C-47s and by the beginning of 1954, the first 10 Westland S-51 Dragonfly helicopters were introduced into active service. In the following period between

1955–1957, the YAF was strengthened with 22 reconnaissance Lockheed RT-33As and 43 Canadair F-86E Sabre interceptors, in which YAF pilots managed for the first time, to break the sound barrier in July 1956. The delivery of 800 various piston engines enabled the Yugoslavs to finish some of their indigenous projects such as Ikarus S-49C or 214, Utva 213, amongst others.[13]

A new section of the Air Force was formed in 1953 when surveillance radars started to enter YAF service. With further deliveries of AN/TPS-1D, AN/TPS-10 and AN/FPS-8 radars in

1954–1955, the surveillance branch expanded to an early-warning system that covered all of Yugoslav airspace.[14]

The Yugoslav Navy was also included in the MDAP. But the programme's influence was much smaller than with the JNA's ground forces or the Air Force. Purchases included artillery, anti-submarine and mine equipment, including ship-borne guns of 30mm, 44mm, 76mm and 127mm calibre, depth charges, mine launchers and anti-submarine mines. To add to this inventory, ammunition for shipboard machineguns and cannons in calibres ranging from 12.7mm to 127mm were issued, coupled with communications equipment, radars, reflectors, engines, electronics and a whole list of smaller items which found their uses in the Yugoslav shipyards.[15] Part of the purchases for the Yugoslav Navy was realised through the so-called 'Off shore' programme which was developed by the Americans during the Korean War for freeing up the capacity of their own military industries. According to this programme, several European military industries were producing different equipment for export within the MDAP framework, or for their own needs also through the same programme. Technical and manufacturing documentation, plus all expenses, were covered by the United States. Several vessels were obtained through this programme, including from France a *Le Fougeux* class patrol boat that entered Yugoslav inventory as '581' and three mine sweepers of the *Ham* class, known in Yugoslavia as type 151. Shipyards at Trogir and Lošinj built *Sirius* class minesweepers, or as the Yugoslavs called them, type 141.[16]

At the request of US and NATO military representatives, the first Yugoslav units which received MDAP equipment were those which belonged to the Fifth Military District and the Yugoslav Air Force. The Fifth Military district was crucial to the broader defence planning of NATO. Here, in the so-called Ljubljana Gap, a Soviet and satellite armies attack was expected. Those units were first to be re-equipped with MDAP supplied armaments.[17]

The Balkan Pact

Yugoslavia's joining the MDAP programme was a significant change of direction for its defence policy. It became almost a part of NATO, through the deliveries of large amounts of military equipment and armaments, the possibility of training its personnel abroad and by the formal introduction of Yugoslavia in NATO war-planning. The other facet of Yugoslavia's siding with the West, was the Balkan Pact.

The Balkan Pact was somewhat of a win-win situation for both NATO and Yugoslavia. After the civil war in Greece ended in the second part of 1949, Greece and Turkey were invited to join NATO and to strengthen the defence of the Mediterranean. However, both countries were separated from other NATO states, not just by the People's Democracies of Bulgaria and Albania but also Tito's Yugoslavia. For Yugoslavia, siding with neighbouring Greece and Turkey as well, was a significant step to connect itself with potential allies in case of a Soviet invasion. It was very much in the interest of all concerned that a rapprochement take place. During mid-1952, efforts in

this direction, which had been proceeding for some time, received their first publicity.[18]

In the context of the Cominform threat, Yugoslavia now had a peaceful and later allied, southern neighbour, Greece. Both states exchanged military representatives in mid-1951 and continued to organise exchange visits of delegations of senior commanders, mutual talks and over-border cooperation, including the setting of new border markings that was mutually conducted in September 1952. Crucial talks between the three General Staffs occurred in the winter of 1952–1953 when the first real steps were agreed for mutual coordination in case of Soviet aggression.

A treaty of friendship was signed on 28 February 1953 in Ankara.[19] It was welcomed by the NATO allies but the Soviet Satellites criticised this pact in the most severe terms. It was not welcomed by another NATO country, Italy, which had a border problem with Yugoslavia during the same period.[20] Stalin's unexpected death in March and the Trieste Crisis of the autumn of 1953, led to a reduction in Yugoslav enthusiasm for further detailed cooperation with Greece and Turkey, despite the fact that cooperation had begun to be more frequent between all three parties.

Looking at preserved documents, besides several joint meetings of the representatives of the three General Staffs in 1953 and 1954, the only concrete cooperation was planned between Yugoslavia and Greece against Bulgaria in south-eastern Macedonia. This was the so-called 'Strumica direction' for the Ground Forces and for all three Air Forces for combat operations in Thrace and Macedonia.[21]

From NATO's point of view, the Balkan Pact brought together armies of three countries with a strength of more than 70 infantry divisions. This was a significant force level, despite their lack of modern equipment. But the Americans were working on this problem since all three armies enjoyed MDAP assistance. As a collective entity, the three armies were far stronger together than they would have been separately.[22]

One problem was Yugoslav reluctance to share defence plans, order of battles and other information with Greece and Turkey. Another was the desire of Yugoslavia's Balkan partners to get Yugoslavia to join NATO, which Tito and his leadership were against. There was also the political issue of how two NATO members would enter the war if the Soviets or any of the satellites attacked Yugoslavia. Or how would Yugoslavia enter the war if Turkey would be attacked by the Soviets? All these dilemmas meant that while the Balkan Pact was an important step for the defence of south-east Europe, it was mainly of

Units of the 2nd Proletarian Division, somewhere around Prokuplje. This division, with its three rifle regiments, was moved in 1950 to south Serbia, to strengthen the garrisons there, as it was estimated that no threat would come from Greece. (Medija Centar Odbrana)

Yugoslav and Greek officers seen during talks at the mutual border. The old alliance was re-established after a period of belligerence during the Greek Civil War. Communist Yugoslavs and Monarchist Greeks, together with the Turks, became close partners in the Balkan Pact, formed in 1953, as a defence against possible Soviet aggression and a specific part of NATO's southern flank. (Author's Collection)

Marshal Tito with the junior officers of the *Galeb*, seen here during the return leg to Yugoslavia, March 1953. (Medija Centar Odbrana)

relations with the Soviets and their satellites were now behind him. It remains surprising how Stalin, with all his sources of intelligence, did not adequately estimate the composition of the Yugoslav Party leadership. They had accompanied Tito for years before the Second World War and were loyal and proud for their achievements during the war and the revolution. Stalin actually lost the battle with Tito.

The *Galeb* sailed on 9 March 1953, escorted by Royal Navy destroyers on a route from Malta past Gibraltar to Britain. Off Gibraltar, the Yugoslav communist leader was greeted by the Royal Navy fleet stationed there.[24] Despite the fact that Stalin was not a threat anymore, in his talks with British officials and in his answers to the press he repeated that an 'isolated war in Europe is impossible' saying, 'For us it is most important to receive armaments and this is the best guarantee'. Tito later stated that Churchill also shared his views on a general war in Europe and confirmed that Great Britain would enter the war if Yugoslavia was attacked by the Soviets or the satellites.[25]

Tito's visit to Great Britain was a real success as he was welcomed as Britain's wartime ally. It was also important from the British perspective to gain knowledge for the planning of future steps to combat the Soviet and satellite threat. Meanwhile, Yugoslavia continued to receive MDAP supplied armaments including the first jets, which arrived on 10 March 1953, during Tito's trip to Britain. Most important to Tito was that there was no Stalin anymore.

a political and diplomatic nature, with only minor mutual concrete steps to counter expected Soviet aggression.[23]

Stalin's Death Relieves Tito from Pressure

In March 1953, Marshal Tito sailed for Great Britain where he would meet Queen Elizabeth II, his wartime acquaintance Prime Minister Winston Churchill and all British officialdom who would give him a splendid welcome. During his travel to the coast where he would board the *Galeb* training ship and start his voyage, Tito was informed that Stalin had died on 5 March 1953. It was very important news. Tito probably felt relieved prior to his important visit to wartime ally Great Britain. His main opponent since 1948 was gone. Knowing the structure of the communist world and practice, Tito was doubtless certain that the most difficult times in his

Border Incidents Continued in 1953

Despite expected political changes in Moscow, incidents on the Yugoslav border continued throughout the whole of 1953. At some parts of the borders, they even intensified. As the *Borba* daily newspaper noted, from the beginning of 1953, the number of incidents grew. Between 20 January and 20 April, nearly 500 incidents occurred on all the borders with the People's Democracy states. Numerous cases of firing on Yugoslav border guards and border posts were noted. Such an increase in the number of incidents led to the conclusion made by General Primorac and Colonel

Brajković that 'in the previous period, the number of anti-Yugoslav border provocations made by the Soviet Bloc had been doubled'. A decision was made 'that Yugoslav border guards would open fire in self-defence on the attackers'.[26]

Violations of Yugoslav airspace also continued, still mostly in the Hungarian and Bulgarian sectors. From diplomatic notes, it can be concluded that 26–27 February 1953 was especially dramatic, counting almost 20 sorties violating Yugoslav airspace from Sombor in Vojvodina to Donja Lendava in Slovenia. Different types were identified from MiG-15s to 'two-engined bombers' in one, two, three or four-ship formations. The altitudes were estimated as 5–6,000 metres, entering from 250 metres to six kilometres into Yugoslav airspace. There were more violations in March in the same sector, including a case when a single MiG dived on a Yugoslav *karaula* near Ferdinandovac and fired a single signal rocket near Škrluce and another case when six unguided rockets were fired on farm No. 912 that belonged to the *Crvena zastava* (Red Star) cooperative. The

A distinctive wooden border post in the vicinity of Horgos, on the Yugoslav-Hungarian border, 1952. This sector was guarded by the 8th Company, 33rd Battalion, 23rd Border Regiment. (Medija Centar Odbrana)

Lake Patrol Boat CM-51, seen during a patrol on Ohrid lake towards the borders of Albania. (Medija Centar Odbrana)

air incursions continued into April and May, carried out mostly by MiG-15s.[27]

It was noted that in the first five months of 1953, there were 172 different incidents on the Romanian border.[28] On the Bulgarian border there were 31 incidents. The soldiers at *Karaula* Tri Kladenca, near the village of Osljane, were fired on by Bulgarian border guards for three days (2, 3 and 5 May).[29] The fire from the Bulgarian side continued during May in the Strumica sector. Other incidents included the usual incursion by armed groups (two members captured by the end of the June in the Strumica area) and distributing propaganda materials across the border.[30] Albanians were also active in sending propaganda materials by balloons, mostly to Kosovo and Metohija province. Such materials were discovered in the various parts of the province, even in the most eastern municipalities.[31]

'Acts of Moscow's butchers' was the Yugoslav press headline for the most serious incidents that had happened up to then. On 24 and 25 June, two Yugoslav border guards were killed. One at the Albanian border (24th) and another on the Bulgarian border (25th). Both soldiers were killed in clashes with armed groups that were infiltrated into Yugoslavia. These incidents led to massive protests in many Yugoslav cities.[32]

In the same period, between February and late September, there were nine incidents when Yugoslav border guards were wounded, on all four borders with satellite states, among the many times that they were fired upon by satellite border troops or armed groups. There were also casualties among the members of those groups in September and October 1953.[33]

Yugoslav Foreign Ministry documents showed that the trend of incidents grew in the autumn of 1953, compared to the summer months. These statistics showed that most of the incidents occurred on the Hungarian border (between 102 and 127 per month), then on Romanian (35 to 62), Bulgarian (10 to 30) and Albanian (7 to 22).[34] However, as can be concluded from other sources, the most difficult incidents with casualties and the incursion of armed groups, occurred at the Bulgarian and Albanian borders.

A glimpse of a change in Soviet policy following Stalin's death did start to be visible at the borders between Yugoslavia and the People's Democracy states. First, conferences to note and comment on border incidents were organised at the end of June with Bulgaria and during August, with Hungary and Albania. In the Yugoslav-Bulgarian meeting, only envelopes with lists of incidents were exchanged.[35] Despite the official talks, the incidents were ongoing. During the initial talks in August, there were 21 firings on Yugoslav border guards and four violations of Yugoslav airspace from Hungary.[36] With the Albanians, talks were continued in November 1953, with meetings on both sides in Ohrid and Podgradec, which resulted in an agreement in December, to formally resolve the border incidents.[37] There was even an exchange on 12 December 1953; one Yugoslav NCO who strayed into Bulgarian territory was exchanged for a Bulgarian pilot and his Yak fighter aircraft, who had become lost and landed at Skopjle air base, on the Yugoslav side.[38]

According to Yugoslav statistics for the period between July 1948 and May 1954, there were a total of 7,877 border incidents, including 3,338 firing on Yugoslav soldiers or infrastructure in the border zone, 288 violations of border, 14 killed and 28 wounded border guards, (there were no statistics for the People's Militia), two killed and 10 wounded civilians, 112 provocations of border guards, 24 removal or destruction of Yugoslav border markers, 246 violations of Yugoslav airspace, 130 illuminations of the border zone with searchlights, 13 violations of Yugoslav territorial waters and six arsons.[39] In another official document, it stated that in the same period, there were 51 soldiers, two NCOs and one officer 'killed or wounded'.[40]

The period between 1949 and 1953 was the peak for the security activities of both the UDBA and the KOS. After Stalin's death and Yugoslavia's closer relationship with the United States and NATO, the pressure from the East was eased. This led to changes in both security services including a reduction in personnel and a certain softening of UDBA methods to combat Soviet supporters.[41] On the tenth anniversary of the Yugoslav security services on 12 May 1954, Svetislav Stefanović summarised the casualty toll of all services and branches involved in the defence of Tito's Yugoslavia since 1945. There were 548 KNOJ troops, 337 People's Militia, 85 members of OZNA/UDBA and 17 border guards killed.[42]

On the opposing side, diplomatic notes dispatched to Belgrade by the satellite states in the same period, reveal the number of fatalities amongst their border guards. In 1949, there were five Hungarian soldiers (two on 26 April and others on 14, 21 May and 30 June), in 1950, three Bulgarian soldiers (two on 27 February and one on 14 July) and a single Albanian soldier (28 October) and in 1951, one Romanian NCO and one soldier (6 February, 5 September) and another Albanian soldier (15 January), were killed.[43] The number of killed or wounded members of the different armed groups (labelled by both sides as bandits, spies, or terrorists) that operated across the borders remain unknown.

'Lost' Soviet Jets in Yugoslavia

During the Cominform Crisis, there were several cases of defection to the other side using aircraft, mostly military. In other cases, both sides came into possession of aircraft that inadvertently strayed across the borders.

Defections from Yugoslavia to the East started immediately after the start of the Crisis. On 16 August 1948, recently promoted Major General Pero Popivoda, defected from Zemun/Belgrade airport to Timisoara, Romania, flying a PO-2.[44] A few weeks later, Commander of the 119th Transport Regiment, Lieutenant Colonel Supek and his Chief of Staff, Major Opojević, forced the pilot of one of the regiment's Sche-2 transports to land in Romania. A single Yak-9P was detached to Zemun/Belgrade air base and ordered to be on constant

alert to prevent further desertions. In 1949, there was a defection from Skopjle, where a pilot from the 94th Regiment, escaped to Bulgaria with a Yak-9P and two defections from the 29th Strike Division at Nis, one with an Il-2 and another with a PO-2. In 1951, General Vlado Popivoda joined his brother, defecting in an aircraft with three other crew members.[45]

In the later period of the Crisis, there were also defections in the other direction. Russian sources quoted that a single DOSAAF (a paramilitary sports organisation) aircraft defected from a 'training centre in Vjzanik', in the Ukrainian SSR to Yugoslavia.[46] On 13 March 1952, a single Romanian Air Force Heinkel He-111, serial AG-58, from the 17th Bomber Regiment in Brashova, landed at Zemin/Belgrade airport. Six members of the crew, including the political commissar of the regiment, asked for asylum.[47] Two Romanian Messerschmitt Bf 109s belonging to the 180th Fighter Regiment, based at Lugosh, defected to Yugoslavia on the morning of 5 July 1952. One of them was the regimental chief of the staff. One (No. 363) landed near Petrovac na Mlavi in Eastern Serbia, while the other one (No. 319) landed at Alibunar in Banat. The pilots deliberately separated, force-landed in different zones and asked for political asylum. This incident was later followed by an exchange of diplomatic notes, in which the Romanian side asked that the pilots be returned. The Yugoslavs replied that they were granted political asylum and asked for the return of Bucker Bu-131 (No. 0856) which strayed into Romanian airspace on 10 December 1950.[48]

Much of the later attention was focused on such Soviet jet types that landed in Yugoslavia and were later tested by the Yugoslavs and Americans as well. These were a single Romanian Yak-23 and a Hungarian MiG-15.

How did the MiG and the Yak come into the possession of the Yugoslav Air Force? Hungarian Air Force MiG-15 (No.25), from the 24th Aviation Regiment, was flown by Lieutenant Laszlo Dombi and force-landed on 9 February 1953. The MiG had taken off from Sarmellek air base, south of Lake Balaton. After three hours of flying, Dombi got lost and force-landed in Yugoslavia, damaging the landing gear and part of the wing. In secrecy, the MiG-15 was transferred to Batajnica air base, repaired and assigned to the VOC (Aviation Testing Centre) for trials. The Americans were informed of the incident much later, on 25 June the same year. Another MiG-15 appeared in Yugoslav air space on the night of 18/19 May 1953. The Soviet pilot, named Bondarenko, got lost while flying over Austria and crashed in the vicinity of Zagreb. Bondarenko was taken into

Stripped of any Romanian Air Force markings, this Yakovlev Yak-23 landed in Yugoslavia. It was tested by the VOC (Aviation Testing Centre) at Batajnica and later quietly passed to the USAF and tested at Wright-Patterson AFB. (VOC)

Pilots and ground crew of the Yugoslav VOC at Batajnica pose near the Hungarian MiG-15, in early 1954. (VOC)

custody and the remains of his MiG was sent to the VOC as well. After contact with the Soviet Embassy, Bondarenko was sent back with what was left of his MiG.

Sometime later, another communist guest arrived unexpectedly. On 24 July 1953, a Romanian Air Force pilot, Lieutenant Mihai Diaconu of the 135th Fighter Regiment based at Karansebes air base, landed his Yakovlev Yak-23 jet fighter (No.35) on a local road near Jagodina, in central Serbia. It was reported in Yugoslavian newspapers that the pilot asked for political asylum, after landing on Yugoslavian soil but after receiving medical treatment, Diaconu asked to be returned to Romania.[49]

Meanwhile, the Yugoslavs put his fighter through intensive trials at Batajnica test centre. During late 1953 the Hungarian MiG was repaired. The VOC tested the core features of both planes for several weeks. Test pilots, Captains Vodopivec, Todorović and Prebeg flew 21 sorties, totalling nine hours, in the Yak and six sorties (fewer than five hours) in the MiG.[50]

In mid-October 1953, the Yak-23 was passed to the USAF for further trials. A Douglas C-124 Globemaster cargo plane arrived at Belgrade with a group of USAF technicians. They took the Romanian Yak with a group of YAF technical staff to the Air Technical Intelligence Centre at Wright-Patterson AFB, Ohio. The trials with the USAF took place during November 1953 with eight sorties, including aerial combat with a North American F-86 Sabre. The Yak was flown by Captain Harold 'Tom' Collins who had also tested a defected North Korean MiG-15 in Okinawa a month earlier. The Yak was dubbed the Bell X-5 Flora and marked as USAF FU-599. These were the first trials of a Soviet jet fighter in the continental

United States. On 30 November, it was returned inside of C-124 to the 'cooperative owner in Eastern Europe'. These tests have remained a secret of American aviation history more than 40 years. Both fighters remained at Batajnica until the spring of 1954 and were then returned to their previous users.[51]

Further Organisational Changes

The first phase of Yugoslavia's new relationship with the United States and NATO brought another tranche of organisational changes to the Yugoslav Army but many of these changes were structural. Becoming almost a NATO member, the Yugoslav Army adopted many changes that took them far from its origin as an ideological army during the turbulent years after 1945.

As part of the reorganisation ordered in 1952, reflecting the MDAP programme and situation on the borders, instead of 'front' as the largest ground forces unit to be created in case of war, now there were three 'operational groups' with HQs to be formed in Ljubljana, Belgrade and Skopjle. The KNOJ was downsized and all existing border regiments became brigades. Outside of the plan, some reorganisation was carried out because of the arrival of new MDAP supplied equipment. Some of the new aviation, artillery, tank, logistical units were formed for this reason and infantry divisions in the Fifth Military District adopted a new organisational structure once they received MDAP armaments. Technical services at the level of the whole army was formed, by excluding the technical elements from different branches. Within the Air Force, all ground Air Force units stationed at one air base now became organised into a single air base, units in the eastern part of Yugoslavia were organised into the newly established VII Aviation Corps. Two existing parachute battalions now became the 63rd Air Landing Brigade. In the Navy, the 1st Escadre was formed by merging squadrons of destroyers

Marshal Tito inspects the Hungarian Air Force MiG-15 at Batajnica air base, January 1954. (Author's Collection)

The relaxed atmosphere within Yugoslav military and political circles was obvious after re-establishing good relations with the Allies, the inclusion into the MDAP programme and Stalin's death. Here, at Batajnica air base, 21 May 1953, Marshal Tito exchanging jokes with (left to right) Foreign Minister Koča Popović, Chief of the General Staff General Peko Dapčević, Minister of Defence General Ivan Gošnjak, assistant to MoD for political issues General Otmar Kreačić and member of Yugoslav Communist Party Politburo Milovan Djilas. In the background are S-49A fighters of the 44th Fighter Division. (Medija Centar Odbrana)

A unique feature of the Yugoslav River Flotilla was the *Sava* monitor. Built in 1906 as the *Bodrog*, she served in the river flotillas of Austria-Hungary, the Kingdom of Yugoslavia, the Independent State of Croatia and Socialist Yugoslavia, until 1962. Nowadays, she can be seen at the Belgrade dockyard. (Medija Centar Odbrana)

Old allies and adversaries from the 'Race to Trieste' in 1945, Chief of the British Imperial Staff, Field Marshal John Harding and Marshal Tito, together at a large JNA manoeuvre near Zagorje, September 1953. (Medija Centar Odbrana)

(6th), patrol boats (38th), torpedo boats (11th and 76th), minelayers (16th) and landing vessels (12th). The first submarine unit with two submarines was also formed.[52] The Counterintelligence Service, KOS, lost 1,400 of its personnel, reducing them from 3,800 (1949) to 2,400 (1952), mostly by losing administrative and cypher personnel.[53]

In mid-January 1953, following a huge state apparatus reorganisation, the Minister of People's Defence was renamed the State Secretary for People's Defence. Tito relieved himself of the minister's duties, retaining only the title of 'Supreme Commander' as President of Yugoslavia. General Gošnjak, who was his Deputy Minister for defence, now became State Secretary for People's Defence with two undersecretaries. The military districts, Air Force, Navy and HQs of Border Troops and Guards were subordinated to the State Secretariat for People's Defence. The General Staff as part of State Secretariat, maintained control over its departments.[54] The Chief of General Staff since autumn 1945, General Koca Popovic, now became State Secretary for Foreign Affairs as a civilian. He was succeeded by his deputy, General Peko Dapčević.[55]

Other changes included disbanding the Main Inspectorate on 5 January 1953.[56] In a new law on military service, conscripts' service was reduced from three to two years, except in the Navy and for students to 18 months. There were further changes in military uniforms, adding three NCO and one new officer ranks.[57] Finally, on 1 June 1953, political commissars ceased to exist in the Yugoslav Army. Ideological dualism between commander and political commissar in the units was abandoned. It was an important step in the de-ideologisation of the Yugoslav Army.[58]

The key unit which sustained the 'small war' on Yugoslavia's borders during the Cominform Crisis, the KNOJ, was disbanded in 1953. Its HQ in central Belgrade, became Command of the Border units, maintaining control over all the border units that earlier belonged to the KNOJ. Other units for interior purposes were all disbanded.[59]

Towards the End of the Cominform Crisis

It is difficult to precisely assign a date for the end of the Cominform Crisis. Stalin's death did not immediately lead to an end of the Crisis. The small war on Yugoslavia's borders continued throughout the whole of 1953 and to a lesser extent, it continued in 1954/55, mostly at the Albanian border where clashes continued. Changes in Moscow led other Soviet Satellites to moderate their policy towards Tito's Yugoslavia.

The sudden outbreak of the so-called Trieste Crisis in the autumn of 1953, redirected Yugoslav attention. The crisis over Trieste culminated in October 1953, when the Allies decided to pass authority over Zone A, which included the city of Trieste itself, to Italy and to withdraw their military contingent. Such a sudden decision provoked one of the most serious Yugoslav military reactions of the Cold War. The movement towards the Italian border by Yugoslav troops was swift. It proved excellent for morale and confirmed the nation's capability to fight, with many problems being overcome. Moreover, the crisis of 1953 hampered relations with the NATO allies, just at the same time as Yugoslavs were negotiating for an improved position in the framework of the MDAP and further partnerships. After the Trieste Crisis reached its end, Western efforts to invite and include Tito's Yugoslavia into NATO's framework slowly vanished, even though Yugoslavia received armaments and equipment through the MDAP for several years more.

The Trieste Crisis of the autumn of 1953 just fuelled Tito's notion that full trust in the capitalist West was not an option. On the other side, he started to react to the first signs of normalisation from Moscow and other communist capitals. A slow process of re-activation of political, economic and even some military-diplomatic contacts began. Finally, in 1955, Soviet Communist Party Secretary General Nikita Khrushchev visited Belgrade and at the airport, immediately after the landing, he read a formal apology for Stalin's attack in 1948. The Cominform Crisis was formally over. Marshall Tito was recognised as the winner.

Members of No 27 Squadron RAF seen here in 1954 at Batajnica air base, during their promotional tour for the English Electric Canberra bomber. (Medija Centar Odbrana)

The final scene of the Cominform Crisis; Soviet Party General Secretary Nikita Khrushchev reads a formal apology from the Soviet Party to the Yugoslav Communist Party, Zemun/Belgrade airport, 1955. Note the difference in dress code of the Yugoslavs (left) and Soviet party leadership (right). Marshal Tito dominates the scene. (Medija Centar Odbrana)

APPENDIX
YUGOSLAV ARMY ORDER OF BATTLE, LATE 1950

Ministry of People's Defence

Different academies and schools, military institutions and enterprises, units that were subordinated to schools and academies, fortification units, radio-companies
398th Communications Regiment – Belgrade

(General Staff)

Guards HQ – Belgrade
4th Guards Division – Belgrade
118th Guards Special Regiment – Belgrade-Dedinje

First Military District – Belgrade (HQ of Front 'G' in case of war)

IV Rifle Corps – Kragujevac
12th Rifle Division – Valjevo
16th Rifle Division – Smederevska Palanka
28th Rifle Division – Zajecar
53rd Rifle Division – Uzice
54th Rifle Division – Pozarevac
52nd Mountain Brigade – Raska
(114th Rifle Division R)
(120th Rifle Division R)
(127th Rifle Division R)
(130th Rifle Division R)

IX Rifle Corps – Novi Sad
3rd Rifle Division – Sremska Mitrovica
51st Rifle Division – Belgrade
62nd Rifle Division – Pancevo
67th Rifle Division – Backa Topola
(102nd Rifle Division R)
(XIV Rifle Corps R) – Belgrade (to be formed in case of war)
17th Tank Division – Kragujevac (203rd TBde – Smederevo, 252nd TBde-Kragujevac, 115th SP Art. Regiment Smederevska Palanka)

Third Military District – Skoplje (HQ of Front 'B' in case of war)

V Rifle Corps – Skoplje

XIII Rifle Corps – Nis
2nd Proletarian Rifle Division – Bitolj
10th Mountain Division – Pristina
35th Rifle Division – Kumanovo
45th Rifle Division – Leskovac
(35th and 75th Rifle Division R)

XIX Rifle Corps – Kumanovo
24th Rifle Division – Stip
42nd Rifle Division –Kumanovo
50th Rifle Division – Kicevo
44th Mountain Brigade – Strumica
209th Mountain Brigade – Prilep
(V Rifle Corps R) – Skoplje (to be formed in case of war)
26th Tank Division – Skoplje (211st TBde Nis, 243rd TBde – Skoplje)

Fifth Military District – Zagreb (HQ of Front 'C' in case of war)

X Rifle Corps – Zagreb
6th Proletarian Rifle Division – Karlovac
30th Rifle Division – Varazdin
56th Rifle Division – Bjelovar
58th Rifle Division – Osijek
(85th and 137th Rifle Division R)

XXIII Rifle Corps – Ljubljana
1st Proletarian Rifle Division – Postojna
33rd Rifle Division – Radgona
60th Rifle Division – Ilirska Bistrica
345th Mountain Brigade – Kranj
(129th Rifle Division R)
20th Tank Division – Sisak (232nd TBde – Jastrebarsko, 265th TBde-Izola, 268th TBde – Vrhnika)
Odred JA – Free Territory of Trieste

Seventh Military District – Sarajevo

XVI Rifle Corps – Tuzla
15th Rifle Division – Tuzla
22nd Rifle Division – Slavonska Pozega
58th Rifle Division – Osek
(171st Rifle Division R)

XXI Rifle Corps – Mostar
25th Mountain Division – Knin
47th Mountain Division – Trebinje
26th Mountain Brigade – Mostar
(111th and 122nd Rifle and 126th Mountain Division R)
219th Tank Brigade – Capljina

Jugoslovensko ratno vazuduhoplovstvo (Yugoslav Air Force) – Zemun
103rd Recce Regiment – Pancevo (Spitfire, Yak-9P)
119th Transport Regiment – Zemun/Belgrade (Ju-52, Li-2 and other types)
322nd Communications Regiment – Zemun

III Mixed Air Corps – Zagreb
21st Mixed Aviation Division – Zemunik/Zadar (Bf 109G, Pe-2)
32nd Bomber Aviation Division – Pleso/Zagreb (Pe-2)
37th Strike Aviation Division – Cerklje (Il-2)
34th Air Technical Command – Zagreb
29th Strike Aviation Division – Nis (Il-2)

39th Fighter Aviation Division – Skoplje (Yak-3, Yak-9P)
44th Fighter Aviation Division – Zemun/Belgrade (S-49A)
41st Air Technical Command – Skoplje
43rd Air Technical Command – Mostar
48th Air Technical Command – Novi Sad
Military Air Academy – Mostar
(Other schools, logistical, technical, medical and other institutions)

Jugoslovenska ratna mornarica – **(Yugoslav Navy) Split**
  11th Torpedo Boat Squadron – Reka
  16th Minelayers Squadron – Losinj
  22nd Auxiliary Ships Detachment – Split
  River Flotilla – Sabac
  5th Naval Zone – Pula
  8th Naval Zone – Sibenik
  9th Naval Zone – Kumbor
  14th Naval Zone – Ploce
  12th Coastal Fortified Section – Island of Vis
  3rd Landing Detachment (466th and 472nd Landing Brigade and
12th Landing Detachment)
  Military Naval Academy – Divulje
(Other schools, logistical, technical, medical and other institutions)

Korpus narodne odbrane Jugoslavije – **Beograd**
Interior forces:
  7th Division NO – Sarajevo
  11th Division NO – Kragujevac
  16th Division NO – Zagreb
  27th Division NO – Novi Sad
Border units:
  436th Border Brigade – Ljubljana
  476th Border Brigade – Skoplje
  23rd Border Regiment – Stari Becej
  199th Border Regiment – Podravska Slatina
  229th Border Regiment – Knjazevac
  31st Naval Border Detachment – Split
  9th Independent Border Battalion – Titograd

BIBLIOGRAPHY

Archival Sources

Arhiv Jugoslavije (Archive of Yugoslavia): fonds: 130, SIV and 507, Arhiv CK SKJ

Diplomatski Arhiv Ministarstva spoljnih poslova (Diplomatic Archive of Ministry of Interior): fonds: PA, *poverljivo 1945–1954* and PA, *strogo poverljivo 1945–1954*

Muzej Jugoslovenskog ratnog vazduhoplovstva (Yugoslav Air Force Museum): fond: RV i PVO

The National Archives (UK): Foreign Office FO 371

Vojni arhiv (Military Archive): fonds: JNA, NOR and VBA

Published Sources

Dokumenti o spoljnoj politici SFRJ; 1945, vol.2; 1946, vol.1–2, 1947, vol.1–2 and 1948, (Belgrade: SSIP, 1984–1986)

Dokumenti o spoljnoj politici SFRJ 1950, edited by Dragan Bogetić and Đoko Tripković, (Belgrade: SMIP, 1993)

Balkanski pakt, zbornik dokumenata (Belgrade: VINC, 2005)

Josip Broz Tito, *Govori i članci* knjige 4-8, (Zagreb: Rad, 1959)

Yugoslav Army Brochures, Bulletins, Manuals, Regulations and Published Orders

Obaveštajna služba i vojnoobaveštajna služba Grčke, (Uprava bezbednosti DSNO. poverljivo, br. evidencije 2309. 1969)

Obaveštajna služba i vojnoobaveštajna služba Mađarske, DSNO, (Uprava bezbednsoti, poverljivo, broj evidencije 1711, 1970)

Obavestajna sluzba SAD, (Uprava Bezbednosti DSNO, poverljivo, broj evidencije 5921, 1968)

Pravilo službe Jugoslovenske narode armije, Službeno (1957)

Zbirka propisa JNA, 3. izmenjeno i dopunjeno izdanje, (Beograd: 1952)

Edition: cija *Razvoj oružanih snaga SFRJ 1945-1985*: knjige 3, *Kopnena Vojska, tom I-III; 4, RV i PVO; 5, Ratna Mornarica; 7, SSNO, tom I-II; 9, Pozadina, tom I-III; 10, Vojno školstvo JNA; 12, Vojna bezbednost; 13, Vojnoobaveštajna služba; 16, Naučnoistraživačka i razvojna delatnost, tom I-II; 17, Tehnicko snabdevanje; 24, Rukovodeći kadar oružanih snaga*, (Beograd: VIZ, 1986-1991)

Military Magazines

Yugoslav: *Službeni list MNO DFJ, Službeni vojni list, Narodna armija, Front, Krila armije, Čuvar Jadrana, Jugoslovenski mornar, Gardist, Za domovinu, Za pobedu, Narodni vojnik, Narodni borac, Narodna milicija, Narodna odbrana, Vojnopolitički glasnik*

Bulgarian: *B'lgarski voin, Narodna voiska, Narodna armia, Voenen propagandist*

Other Magazines

Borba, Vojska, Aeroplan, Aeromagazin, Wheels and Tracks, Flying, Mornarički glasnik, Glasnik RV i PVO

Scientific and Other Articles

Bisenić Dragan, 'Sveočenje Vladimira Velebita', *Politika* March–April 2001

Harold Bourgeois, 'Tito's Jet Jockeys – Three Yugoslav combat veterans are learning jet techniques, Yankee style', *Flying*, (July 1953), pp.28–29 and 46

Dabović Krsto, 'Stvaranje i razvoj pozadine Ratnog vazduhoplovstva i protivvazdušne odbrane', *Glasnik RV i PVO*, 2/1972 (Belgrade: 1972)

Dimitrijević Bojan, 'Yugoslav-Soviet Military Relations 1945–1948', *The Journal of Slavic Military studies*, vol.9, no.3, September 1996, pp.581–593

Dimitrijević Bojan, 'The Mutual Defence Aid Programme in Tito's Yugoslavia 1951–1958 and its Technical Impact', *The Journal of Slavic Military Studies*, vol.10, no.2, June 1997, pp.19–33

Heuser Beatrice, 'Yugoslavia in Western Military Planning 1948–53', in Marko Milivojević (ed.), *Yugoslavia's Security Dilemas* (New York: Berg, 1988)

'Ekspoze general-pukovnika Ivana Gošnjaka u narodnoj skupštini FNRJ o Vojnom budžetu za 1952', *Vojnopolitički glasnik*, 2/1952

'Kazivanja narodnog heroja general-pukovnika u penziji Blaža S. Jankovića: Inžinjerija JNA od 1948 do 1955', *Narodna armija*, April 1990

Koliševski Lazar, 'Tito i moja generacija', *NIN*, 18. jun 1989, p.2

Micevski Milan, 'Neustrašivi lovac, Avion Jak-9P', *Specijalno izdanje magzina Odbrana, Arsenal br.31*, 15 July 2009

Micevski Milan, 'Jugoslovebski Gustavi, Razvoj varijanti lovačkih aviona Meseršmit Bf 109', *Specijalno izdanje magzina Odbrana, Arsenal br.49*, 15 January 2011

Micevski Milan, 'Branilac prestonice, lovacki avion Ikarus S-49A', *Posebno izdanje lista Odrabana: Arsenal br.9*, 15 September 2007

Micevski Milan 'Poslednji domaci lovac: avion Ikarus S-49C', *Posebno izdanje lista Odrabana: Arsenal br.19*, 15 July 2008

Micevski Milan and Dimitrijevic Bojan, *Balkan Mosquitos, Flypast*, November 1990

kapetan Milojević Miodrag, 'Naša industrija motornih vozila', *Tenkovski glasnik* 3/1950

Oštrić Šime-Ognjan Petrović, 'Avia S-92 Turbina', *Aeroplan July-August 1989*, br.4, pp.18–21

Oštrić Šime, 'Esovi-potomci Ika', *Aviorevija, br 10*, oktobar 1983, p.20

Pribilović Kažmir, 'Pomorske snage Jugoslovenske ratne mornarice 1945. godine', *Mornarički glasnik, -7/1986*, pp.693–705

Radić Aleksandar, 'Staljinova dalekometna artiljerija, Top T-122mm i haubica 152mm', *Specijalno izdanje magzina Odbrana, Arsenal br.47*, 15 November 2011

Radić Aleksandar, *Povratak Škoda, Češka vozila u našoj vojsci*, Specijalno izdanje magzina Odbrana, Arsenal br. 58, 15. oktobar 2011

Ristović Milan, 'Mali rat' na Jugoslovensko-grčkoj granici (1945-1950)', *Vojnoistorijski glasnik* 3/1999

Ristović Milan, 'Eksperiment Buljkes', *Godišnjak za društvenu istoriju* IV/2-3 1997, pp.179–186

Roganović Mirko, '30 godina jedinica VOJIN', *Glasnik RV i PVO*, 3/83

General-Major Roglić Stevan, 'Rađanje našeg RV i PVO', *Glasnik RV i PVO*, 2/1972

Stanišić Milija, 'Kadrovska komponenta učešća Crne Gore u NOR-u (1941-1945)', *Istorijski zapisi*, godina XXXIV (LIV) 3–4

Stojić Jovan, 'Na svetlim tradicijama 254. lovačkog puka', *Glasnik RV i PVO*, 3/1978

Ulepič Zdenko, general-pukovnik u penziji, 'Posleratni razvoj jugoslovenskog ratnog vazduhoplovstva i protivvazdušne odbrane', *Glasnik RV i PVO*, 2/1972

Životić Aleksandar, 'Referat sovjetskog pukovnika Ktitorenka o reorganizaciji Jugoslovenske armije', *Tokovi istorije* 3/2007, pp.209–216

Životić Aleksandar, 'Zašto je reorganizovana Jugoslovenska armija 1948? Ratni plan Maksimum', *Istorija 20. veka* 1/2008, pp.57–70

Monographs

Anić, Nikola-Joksimović Sekula-Gutić Mirko, *Narodno oslobodilačka vojska Jugoslavije* (Belgrade: VIZ, 1982)

Anon, *Bela knjiga o agresivnim postupcima vlada SSSR, Poljske, Čehoslovačke, Mađarske, Rumunije, Bugarske i Albanije prema Jugoslaviji* (Belgrade: MIP FNRJ, 1951)

Anon, *Enciklopedija Jugoslavije*, vol.1, (Zagreb: Leksiografski zavod, 1955)

Anon, *Trideset godina Školskog centra PVO* (Zadar: SC PVO, 1975)

Anon, *35 godina rada Atomsko-biloško-hemijske odbrane* (Belgrade: SC ABHO, 1980)

Antić, Boško, *Podmornice* (Belgrade: NIU Vojska, 1996)

Babić, Manojlo, *Vrhovni komandant među tenkistima* (Belgrade: VIZ, 1982)

Babić, Milenko, and Mihailo, Saranović, *Enver Hodžina Albanija.* (Beograd: Tanjug, 1981)

Banac, Ivo, *Sa Staljinom protiv Tita* (Zagreb, Globus, 1990)

Bekić, Darko, *Jugoslavija u hladnom ratu* (Zagreb, Globus, 1988)

Bjelica, Obrad, *Vojna akademija kopnene vojske 1944–1984* (Belgrade: VIZ, 1983)

Čuvari našeg neba (Belgrade: VIZ, 1977)

Dedijer, Vladimir, *Novi prilozi za biografiju Josipa Broza Tita*, tom.1 (Zagreb-Rijeka: Mladost, Spektar, Liburnija, 1980)

Dedijer, Vladimir, *Novi prilozi za biografiju Jospia Broza Tita*, tom.3 (Belgrade: Rad, 1984)

Dimitrijevic, Bojan & Micevski Milan, *JETS, avioni americkog porekla u jugoslovenskom naoružanju 1953–1974* (Belgrade: Spektar, 1991)

Đorgović, Momčilo, *Đilas vernik i jeretik* (Belgrade: private edition, 1989)

Đukić, Slavoljub, *Čovek u svom vremenu, Razgovori sa Dobricom Ćosićem* (Belgrade: Filip Visnjic, 1989)

Hodža, Enver, *Titoisti, Prevod za internu upotrebu PCKSKJ – Sektor za IPD* (Belgrade: 1982)

Janić, Čedomir upravnik Muzeja JV, *70 godina vazduhoplovne industrije Jugoslavije 1923–1993*, katalog za istoimenu izložbu (Belgrade: MJV, 1993)

Jakšić, Pavle, *Nad uspomenama*, drugi deo (Belgrade: Rad, 1990)

Janković, Milorad, *Tenkovi, juče i danas* (Belgrade: VIZ, 1984)

Jovanović, S. Aleksandar, *Poraz, koreni poraza* (Belgrade: 2001)

Jovanovic, Leonid, *Tehnicka sluzba KoV JNA 1945–1985* (Belgrade: VIZ, 1989)

Jović, Stojan, *Istorija jugoslovenskog padobranstva* (Belgrade: Gornji Milanovac, 1996)

Jugoslovensko-sovjetski sukob 1948 (Belgrade: ISI, 1999)

Kampanja protv FNRJ 1948–1958, za službenu upotrebu (Uprava za moralno-političko vaspitanje JNA, oktobar 1958)

Kardelj, Edvard, *Sećanja – Borba za priznanje i nezavisnost nove Jugoslavije 1944-57*, (Ljubljana: Belgrade, Radnicka stampa, 1980)

Kljakić, Dragan, *Izgubljena pobeda generala Markosa* (Belgrade: Narodna knjiga, 1987)

Kolo, Aleksandar & Dimitrijević, Bojan, *Spitfajer* (Belgrade: Aero Art, 1997)

Laković, Ivan, *Zapadna vojna pomoć Jugoslaviji 1951–1958*, (Podgorica: Istorijski institut Crne Gore, 2006)

Lazarević, Božo, *Vazduhoplovstvo u NOR u 1941–1945* (Belgrade: VIZ, 1972)

Ličina, Đorđe, *Izdaja* (Zagreb: CIP, 1985)

Marković, J. Predrag, *Belgrade između Istoka i Zapada 1948–1965* (Belgrade: Sluzbeni list SRJ, 1996)

Milatović, Arso, *Pet diplomatskih misija*, 1-2, (Ljubljana: Cankarjeva Zalozba, 1985)

Miljković, Mita, *Burne diplomatske godine, iz sofijskog denvnika 1953–1956* (Belgrade: Sluzbeni glasnik, 1995)

Nikolić, B. Drago, *Razvoj političkih organa u Jugoslovenskoj narodnoj armiji* (Belgrade: VIZ, 1985)

Oružane snage Jugoslavije 1941–1981 (Belgrade: VIZ, 1982)

Pljaku, Panajot, *Nasilje nad albanskom revolucijom* (Belgrade: Narodna knjiga, 1984)

Petranović, Branko, *Jugoslavija na razmeđu (1945–1950)* (Podgorica: CANU, 1998)

Pezo, Omer, *Vojna industrija Jugoslavije* (Belgrade: VIZ, 1983)

Miroslav, Popović, *Udri bandu* (Belgrade: Filip Visnjic, 1986)

Popović, B. Nikola, *Jugoslovensko-sovjetski odnosi u Drugom svetskom ratu* (Belgrade: ISI, 1988)

Pribilović, Kažmir, *Naoružani brodovi Mornarice NOVJ* (Split: VPO, 1980)

Radonjić, Radovan, *Izgubljena orijentacija* (Belgrade: 1985)

Rendulić, Zlatko, *Avioni domaće konstrukcije posle Drugog svetskog rata* (Belgrade: 1996)

Stevanović Milivoje, *U Titovim fabrikama 'izdajnika'* (Belgrade: Kultura, 1991)

Terzić, Milan (ed.), *Balkanski pakt 1953–1954*, edited by (Belgrade: Medija centar, 2008)

Tito, Josip Broz, *Stvaranje i razvoj Jugoslovenske armije* (Belgrade: Glavna politicka uprava 1949)

Vasić, Borislav, *Avioni jugoslovenskog neba* (Belgrade: 1987)

Vojni leksikon (Belgrade: VIZ, 1981)

Vukadinović, Dušan & Vejnović, Glišo, *Centar visokih vojnih škola JNA 'Maršal Tito'* (Belgrade: VIZ, 1983)

Vukmanović, Svetozar-Tempo, *Revolucija koja teče, Memoari*, (Belgrade: Komunist, 1971)

Živanović, Miljenko, *Centar vojnih škola kopnene vojske 1945–1985* (Belgrade: VIZ, 1989)

Žutić, Nikola, *Ikarus-Ikarbus 1923–1998*, (Belgrade: BMG-Ikarbus, 1999)

Životić, Aleksandar, *Jugoslavija, Albanija i velike sile 1945–1961* (Belgrade: Arhipelag 2011)

NOTES

Chapter 1

1   Roumen Daskalov, *Debating the Past, Modern Bulgarian History: From Stambolov to Zhivkov*, (Budapest–New York: CEU Press, 2011), pp.229, 246.

Chapter 2

1   Vojni arhiv Ministarstva odbrane Republike Srbije (Military Archive of the Ministry of Defence, Belgrade, further as: VA), fond JNA, k. 49, f.8, 2/1 and f.3, 10/1; *Službeni list Minstartsva narodne odbrane Demokratske Federativne Jugoslavije* (MNO DFJ), pp.10–11.; 'Novi zakon o demobilizaciji', *Narodna armija*, 30. 10. 1945, p.4.

2   The National Archives (UK), FO 371, 48898, R 16611/445/92 and 48871, R 16798/130/92.

3   'Naše jedinice ispraćaju demobilisane drugove', *Narodna armija*, 1.12.1946, p.7.

4   'U jedinicama se vrše pripreme za odlazak demobilisanih boraca', *Narodna armija*, 17. 11. 1945. p.5; 'Uspešno završena demobilizacija po Zakonu od 20 oktobra', *Narodna armija*, 1.1. 1946, p.5.

5   'Naredba Br. 10 VKOS i MNO FNRJ za 22. Septembar 1946 godine', *Narodna armija*, 5. 10.1946. p.1.

6   'O prestojećem upućivanju regruta u stalni kadar', *Narodna armija*, 23. 11. 1946, p.1; See whole page 6 in *Narodna armija*, 30. 11. 1946.

7   *Službeni list MNO DFJ*, 1–2/1946, pp.1–5. 'Zakon o službi u Jugoslovenskoj armiji', *Narodna armija*, 20. 7. 1946, p.1.

8   *Zakon o sluzbi u Jugoslovenskoj armiji, Zbrika propisa JNA*, Third revised edition (Belgrade: 1952), p.63.

9   *Vojnopoliticki glasnik* (Belgrade 4/1949), p.35.

10   Milovan Djilas, 'Naša armija, kovacnica novih ljudi', *Borba*, 20. 8. 1946; Pukovnik Vjekoslav Kolb, 'Povodom demobilizacije nove partije obveznika', *Narodna armija*, 8. 10. 1946. 1, p.1.

11   *Za domovinu*, No. 49, 31 February 1949.

12   *Narodni vojnik*, 64, 20 November 1949.

13   'Za ideologicheskata podgotovka na oficirite', *Voenen propagandist*, 5 May 1948, p.21.

14   *Oružane snage Jugoslavije 1941–1981*, (B 223; Mile S. Bjelajac, *Jugoslovensko iskustvo sa mulitetničkom armijom 1918–1991*, Beograd 1999. 47.

15   *Oružane snage Jugoslavije 1941–1981*, (Belgrade: VIZ, 1982), pp.223, 228.

16   *Front*, 61, 1. 1. 1948; Razvoj OS SFRJ 1945–1985, vol.24, *Rukovodeći kadar oružanih snaga*, (Belgrade: VIZ 1990). 27–57.

17   Milija Stanišić, 'Kadrovska komponenta učešća Crne Gore u NOR-u (1941–1945)', *Istorijski zapisi*, XXXIV (LIV) 3–4, (Titograd 1981), p.37.

18   *Vojni leksikon*, (Beograd: VIZ 1981), second part which contains the biographies of the JNA generals.

19   Bojan Dimitrijević, 'Pobuna jugoslovenske periferije, Generalski kor Jugoslovenske armije 1945–1953', *Zbornik radova sa naučnog skupa Dijalog povijesničara–istoričara*, No 7, (Zagreb: Fridrich Nauman Stifftung, 2003), pp.287–306.

20   Bogdan Radica, *Hrvatska 1945*, (Minhen–Barcelona: 1974), pp. 55 and pp.184–185.

21   Bojan Dimitrijević, 'Armija i jugoslovenski identitet 1945–1992 godine', *Vojno delo* 2/2001, pp.141–154.

22   Pavle Jakšić, *Nad uspomenama*, drugi deo, (Beograd: Rad, 1990), pp.26–27.

23   *Razvoj OS SFRJ 7–1, SSNO II*, (Beograd, VIZ 1990), pp.15–24, 38–77; Jakšić, *Nad uspomenama*, pp.26–27, 54–56.

24   VA, fond NOR, k. 49, f. 2–3/1; f.4, k. 23, f. 1–17 and k.25A, f–2/I, 21 ('Skica vojnoteritorijalne podele Jugoslavije'); Razvoj OS SFRJ, *3–3 Kopnena vojska* (Beograd: VIZ 1990), p.510.

25   VA, NOB, k. 25A, f–2/I, 38 ('Naređenje za formiranje Komande tenkovskih i motorizovanih jedinica JA, 7. maja 1945'), VA, NOB, k. 591, knjiga 2 k. 593, k.1; Razvoj OS SFRJ 1945–1985, *3–2, Kopnena vojska* (Belgrade 1988), pp.153–154.

26   More details in recent study: Dmitar Tasic, *Korpus narodne odbrane Jugoslavije*, (Belgrade: INIS, 2020).

27   Bojan Dimitrijević, *Jugoslovensko ratno vazdruhoplovstvo 1942-1992* (Belgrade: ISI–MC Odbrana, 2016), pp.52–55.

28   VA, NOR k.1457, 85–87/7; *Razvoj Oružanih snaga SFRJ 1945 –1985, 4, Ratno vazduhoplovstvo i protivvazdušna odbrana*, (Belgrade: VIZ, 1989), pp.43–45; Pukovnik Krsto Dabović, 'Stvaranje i razvoj pozadine Ratnog vazduhoplovstva i protiv vazdušne odbrane, *Glasnik RV i PVO*, (Belgrade, 2/1972), pp.51–56; Kolo Aleksandar i Dimitrijević Bojan, *Spitfajer*, (Belgrade: Aero Art, 1997).

29   Kapetan bojnog broda dr Kažimir Pribilović, 'Pomorske snage Jugoslovenske ratne mornarice 1945.godine', *Mornarički glasnik*, 1986/7, (Spilit, 1986), pp.693–697.

30   VA, JNA, k. 294, f.2, 2/1; Diplomatski arhiv Ministarstva spoljnih poslova (DA MSP), fond PA, 1946, f–44, 21, 675.

31   VA, JNA, k. 294, f.1/4; VA, fond Vojnobezbednosna agencija (Military Security Agency, further as: VBA), k.8, 6.3.03.2, *sveska* (sv.) br.8 ('Izveštaj KOS JRM za 1946–1947')

32   VA, JNA, k. 49, f.2, 20/1; Razvoj OS SFRJ 1945–1985, 3–1. *Kopnena vojska* (Belgrade: VIZ 1988), p.41.

33   VA, JNA, k. 49, f.9, 1/1.

34   'Dva novembra naše garde (II)', *Vojska* (15.11. 2001), p.38.

35   *Oružane snage Jugoslavije 1941–1991*, pp.159. 243; Razvoj OS SFRJ, 3–3, pp.512–513.

36   VA, fond JNA, k.52, f.1 1/26. VA, fond JNA, k.52, f.2 1/3. VA, fond JNA, k.52, f.2 1/1–4.

37   *Istorijat Vojne Akademije za 1945. godinu*. 6–8; Obrad Bjelica, Vojna akademija KoV (Beograd: VIZ, 1983), p.81.

38   'Važnost i uloga oficirskih škola i učilišta – Osvrt na razvoj i perspektive', *Narodna armija*, 1.1.1946, p.2.

39   Bjelica, *Vojna akdemija*, pp.96–101; 'Vesti iz armije', *Narodna armija*, 4. 12. 1945, p.5; Razvoj OS SFRJ 1945–1985, 3–2, pp.160–161.

40   Razvoj OS SFRJ 1945–1985, 3–2, pp.276–277, 410; *Razvoj OS SFRJ 1945–1985*, 3–3, pp.272–276.

41   *Razvoj OS SFRJ 1945–1985*, 4, pp.45, 63; *Vojni leksikon*, pp.598–599 and 662; Dimitrijević, *Jugoslovensko ratno vazdruhoplovstvo 1942–1992*, pp.429–431.

42   Kažimir Pribilović, 'Uz četrdesetogodišnjicu početka rada Vojnopomorskog učilišta JRM', *Mornarički glasnik* 1986, pp.854–862; *Jugoslovenski mornar*, 10/1949.

43   *Razvoj OS SFRJ 7–1, SSNO* (Beograd: VIZ, 1990), p.125.

44   VA, fond: Zatvorena gradja, svezanj (ZG, sv) 1221, *Glavna trofejna baza, monografija jedinice*.

45   VA, ZG, k. 602, 'Štab I TA st. pov 3/45, 13.7.1945'.

46   VA, JNA, k. 49, f.2, 13–14/1; VA, NOB, k. 21, f–1, 19 and k. 25a, 2/I, 40.

47   *Razvoj OS SFRJ 1945-1985,* 17, *Opremanje naoružanjem* (Belgrade: VIZ, 1989), pp.179–180, 200–201 and 252–253.

48   DA MSP, PA, 1945, f 3, 6, 2965, 2495 and f 3, 7, 3278.

49   VA, JNA, k. 287, f 2, 21; Razvoj OS SFRJ, 17, pp.179–180.

50   VA, NOR k. 57, 26/25–2.

51   VA, NOR k. 25A, 20, 2/11.

52   *Čuvari našeg neba* (Belgrade: VIZ, 1977), p.253; Čedomir Janić, upravnik Muzeja JV, *70 godina vazduhoplovne industrije Jugoslavije 1923-1993, catalogue for exhibition;* Nikola Žutić, *Ikarus-Ikarbus 1923-1998,* (Belgrade: 1999), pp.34–36.

53   *Razvoj OS SFRJ,* 4, pp.234–235; Zlatko Rendulić, *Avioni domaće konstrukcije posle Drugog svetskog rata,* (Belgrade: 1996), p.35.

54   VA, NOR k. 25b, 23–4/1.

55   Arhiv Jugoslavije (Archive of Yugoslavia, Belgrade – further as AJ), fond 507 (Arhiv CK SKJ) III–22.

56   *Oružane snage Jugoslavije 1941-1981,* pp.583.

57   VA, JNA, k. 286, f–2, 17/5; *Razvoj OS SFRJ,* 17, p.28; *Oružane snage Jugoslavije 1941-1981,* pp.582–583.

58   Jakšić, *Nad uspomenama,* drugi deo, pp.19.

59   *Dokumenti o spoljnoj politici SFRJ – 1950,* edited by Dragan Bogetić i Đoko Tripković, (Beograd: SSIP, 1993), p.360.

60   Vojni arhiv, fond VBA, k. 17, 6.3.03.3, sv. br.37 and sv. br.38.

61   Bojan Dimitrijević, *Rankovic, drugi covek,* (Beograd: Vukotic media, 2020).

62   VA, VBA, k. 8, f.1.

63   VA, VBA, k. 54, 7.2 and sv. br. 25, 120. 'General Jefto Šašić'.

64   Svetko Kovač – Irena Popović Gligorov, *Vojna služba bezbednosti u Srbiji,* (Belgrade: MC Odbrana 2014). Dmitar Tasic, 'Osnivanje i rad kontraobaveštajne službe u jugoslovenskim oružanim snagama – prilog istraživanju vojne službe bezbednosti' Vojnoistorijski glasnik, (Belgrade 1–2013), pp.200–223.

65   VA, VBA, kl.0.01.01 f. 1 and 4.

66   VA, VBA, k.7, 6.3.02. sv. 7.

67   *Razvoj Oružanih snaga SFRJ 1945-1985,* Vol.13 – *Vojnoobaveštajna služba,* (Beograd: VIZ, 1991), pp.102–106.

68   *Ibid,* pp.106–108.

69   *Ibid,* pp.214–221.

70   *Razvoj Oruzanih snaga SFRJ 1945-1985,* 3–1, pp.40–43 and 48–49; *Oruzane snage Jugoslavije 1941-1981,* p.174.

71   Nikola Popović, *Jugoslovensko-sovjetski odnosi u Drugom svetskom ratu,* (Beograd: ISI, 1988), p.306.

72   *Voenen propagandist,* No.1, June 1947, p.4 and No. 5, September 1947, p.38.

73   VA, NOB, k. 17a, 1–6 and 4–4.

74   Popović, n.d. p.206; VA, NOB, k. 57–2, 24.

75   *Razvoj Oruzanih snaga SFRJ 1945-1985,* 3–2, pp.385–389.

76   *Razvoj Oruzanih snaga SFRJ 1945-1985,* 3–2, pp.414 and 423.

77   *Razvoj Oruzanih snaga SFRJ 1945-1985,* 3–2, pp.22 and 23.

78   Božo Lazarević, *Vazduhoplovstvo u NOR-u 1941-1945,* (Beograd: VIZ, 1972), p.162; Jovan Stojić, 'Na svetlim tradicijama 254.lovačkog puka', *Glasnik RV i PVO,* 3/1978 (Belgrade 1978).

79   Dimitrijević, *Jugoslovensko ratno vazdruhoplovstvo 1942-1992,* pp.45–46; MJRV (Yugoslav Air Force Museum), 'Yugoslav Air Forces serial numbers logbook 1946-1947'.

80   *Razvoj Oruzanih snaga SFRJ 1945-1985,* 3–2, p.156; *Razvoj Oruzanih snaga SFRJ 1945-1985,* 17, *Naoruzanje i oprema* (Belgrade: VIZ 1989), pp.252–253.

81   *Cuvari naseg neba,* pp.252–254.

82   Popović, *Jugoslovensko-sovjetski odnosi u Drugom svetskom ratu,* p.230.

83   VA, JNA, k. 49, f.3, 21/1–3.

84   VA, VBA, k.8, 6.3.02. sv. 12 and k.17, 6.3.03.2, sv.38. 'Uprava KOS JNA, *Desetogodišnji izveštaj, Borba protiv neprijatelja 1944-1954,* maj 1954'.

85   DA MSP, PA, 1946, f–78, 15, 15105, 19, 5510 and 14, 14715; 'Članovi sovjetske misije napustili našu zemlju', *Narodna armija* 8. 10. 1946, p.1; *Narodna armija,* 16. 7. 1946, p.1; *Front,* No 14 20 January 1946; *Front* 58, 21 Novembar 1947.

86   Obrad Bjelica, *Vojna Akademija KoV 1944-1984* (Belgrade: VIZ, 1983), p.82. Leonid Jovanović, *Tehnicka sluzba KoV JNA* (Beograd: VIZ, 1989), p.36; *Razvoj Oruzanih snaga SFRJ 1945-1985,* 3–2, pp.161 and 284.

87   Bjelica, *Vojna Akademija KoV,* pp 79–80 and 82.

88   Miljenko Zivanovic, *Centar Vojnih Skola Kopnene Vojske 1945-1985* (Belgrade: VIZ, 1989). pp 72–76.

89   Bjelica, *Vojna Akademija KoV,* pp 86–94; Zivanovic, *Centar Vojnih Skola,* pp.72–76.

90   Vladimir Dedijer, *The Battle Stalin Lost* (New York: Viking, 1971), p.104.

91   Edvard Kardelj, *Secanja – Borba za priznanje i nezavisnost nove Jugoslavije, 1944-1957* (Belgrade-Ljubljana: Radnicka stampa, 1980), pp.101–102.

92   Zoltan Barany, *Soldiers and politics in Eastern Europe, 1945-1990,* (New York: St Martin Press, 1993), p.48.

93   General Stevan Roglić, 'Radjanje naseg RV i PVO', *Glasnik RV i PVO* 2/72, (Belgrade, 1972). pp 21–27.

94   *Razvoj Oruzanih snaga SFRJ 1945-1985,* 12, p.224. Analyses of the KOS service provides fewer numbers – although numbers differ: 2.395 (estimation in 1950) and 3.140 (1951), VA, VBA k. 9, 6.3.02, sv. 16, 146.

95   *Razvoj Oruzanih snaga SFRJ 1945-1985,* 3–2, pp.189 and 277.

96   Manojlo Babić, *Oklopne jedinice u NOR-u* (Belgrade: VIZ, 1968).

97   Jovanović, *Tehnicka Sluzba KoV JNA,* pp.27 and 87.

98   *Vojni leksikon* (Belgrade: VIZ, 1981), pp.773–1129.

99   Jovan Stojić, Na svetlim tradicijama 254. lovačkog puka, *Glasnik RV i PVO* 3/78, (Belgrade 1978); Božo Lazarević, *Vazduholpvstvo u NOR-u,* Belgrade 1972.

100 Robert Lee Wolf, *The Balkans in our Time* (New York: Norton Library, 1967), p.354.

Chapter 3

1   Daskalov, *Debating the Past,* p.228.

2   VA, NOB, k. 1411, f 4, 39; Branko Petranovic, *Politicka i ekonomska obnova narodne vlasti,* Belgrade 1969, p.179.

3   'Povodom ugovora o prijateljstvu, Tekst ugovora o uzajamnoj pomoći između FNRJ i NR Albanije', *Narodna armija,* 13. 7. 1946, p.3

4   *Razvoj Oruzanih snaga SFRJ 1945-1985,* 4, p.433.

5   *Enver Hodzina Albanija* (Belgrade: TANJUG Yugoslav informative agency, 1981), p.52.

6   Panajot Pljaku, *Nasilje nad Albanskom revolucijom* (Belgrade: Narodna knjiga, 1984), p.57.

7   *Razvoj Oruzanih snaga SFRJ,* 4, p 433; *Enver Hodzina Albaija,* p.52.

8   Arso Milatović, *Pet diplomatskih misija* (Ljubljana: Cankarjeva Zalozba, 1985), vol. I, pp.162–163.

9   AJ, A CK SKJ, IX, 1/IV-27, 109–124; VA, fond JNA, k. 286, f.2, 25/1 and k.287, f.2, 1–24, 37.

10   DA MSP, PA, 1945, f 3, 8, 6319; *Wheels and tracks,* (No. 38, 1992), pp.13–19. AJ, A CK SKJ, IX 1/IV-27, 189.

11 AJ, A CK SKJ, IX, 1/IV–27, 145–176.

12 *Razvoj Oruzanih snaga SFRJ*, 3–II, p.158.

13 AJ ACK SKJ IX 1/IV–27, 184–18; *Enver Hodzina Albanija*, p.52.

14 *Enver Hodzina Albanija*, p.52.

15 Headquarter of the 1st Pilot School to Yugoslav Air Force Command/Training Section, confidential 11/59, 13 February 1959. Document is preserved in Archive of the Yugoslav Air Force Museum at Zemun without any archive markings.

16 List of Albanian Army members that had passed training at II class Air Force Technical Training Centre and testimonies of their Yugoslav colleagues prepared for: *The Yugoslav–Albanian relations White Book* that was published in 1959. Archive of the YAF Museum, without markings.

17 *Razvoj Oruzanih snaga SFRJ*, 3–II, p.161; Mljenko Zivanovic, *Centar Visokih Vojnih Skola KoV 1945–1985*, (Belgrade: VIZ 1989), pp.99–100 and 498.

18 Ratko Niksic, *Istorija 119. vazduhoplovnog transportnog puka* (Unpublished manuscript), p.31.

19 YAF Museum, k. 30, 'History of the 116th fighter aviation regiment', pp.6–7; Milatović, *Pet diplomatskih misija*, p.161.

20 *Enver Hodzina Albanija*, p.52.

21 Pljaku, *Nasilje nad Albanskom revolucijom*, p.56.

22 *Vojni Leksikon*, p.995; *Razvoj Oruzanih snaga SFRJ*, 3–I, p.76.

23 VA, NOR, k. 1374, f. 6, 2.

24 VA, NOR, k. 1308, f. 6, 13.

25 Dragan Kljakic, *Izgubljena pobeda Generala Markosa* (Belgrade: Narodna knjiga, 1987), p.90.

26 Edvard Kardelj, *Secanja – Borba za priznanje i nezavisnost nove Jugoslavije, 1944–1957* (Belgrade–Ljubljana: Radnicka stampa, 1980), p 116.

27 Kljakic, *Izgubljena pobeda Generala Markosa*. p.87 and 188; *Dokumenti o spoljnoj politici SFRJ*, 1947, vol. I, (Beograd: SSIP, 1986), pp.236–237; Milan Ristović, 'Eksperiment Buljkes', *Godišnjak za društvenu istoriju* IV/2–3 1997, pp.179–186.

28 Lazar Koliševski, 'Tito i moja generacija', *NIN* magazine, 18. 6 1989, p.23.

29 *Studies in the history of th Greek Civil War 1945–1949*, p.303.

30 Kljakic, *Izgubljena pobeda Generala Markosa*, pp.191–194.

31 Kljakic, *Izgubljena pobeda Generala Markosa*, pp.281–282.

32 Kljakic, *Izgubljena pobeda Generala Markosa*, pp.113, 120, 131; *Dokumenti*, 1947, vol.II, pp.467–471.

33 Djordje Ličina, *Tragom plave lisice* (Zagreb: CIP 1990), p.267; Kljakic, pp.80–81 and 105; *Dokumenti*, 1947 vol. I, pp.294–300 and 321.

34 DA MSP, PA, 1946, f–30, 4, 10758.

35 *Dokumenti*, 1946, vol.II, pp.50, 318 and 320; *Dokumenti*, 1947, vol.I, p.505; *Dokumenti*, 1947, vol.II, pp.3, 12, 41, 129 and 151; *Dokumenti*,1948, pp.347–348.

36 *Narodna odbrana*, 23, 4. June 1949; DA MSP, PA, 1949, f–39, 19, 39532, 39537, 39549 and f–22, 39686, 39696, 39673 and f–24.

37 Kljakic, *Izgubljena pobeda Generala Markosa*, p.133.

38 Elizabeth Barker, 'Yugoslav Policy towards Greece 1947–1949', pp.281–282 and 290–291 and Jože Pirjavec, 'The Tito-Stalin Split and the End of the Civil War in Greece', pp.314–315, both in: *Studies in the History of the Greek Civil War 1945–1949*, (Copenhagen: Museum Tusculanum Press, 1987).

39 Koliševski, *Tito i moja generacija*.

40 Most recent account in: Kaloyan Matev, *Red Wind over Balkans, The Soviet Offensive South of the Danube, September–October 1944*, (Warwick: Helion and Co, 2019).

41 *Narodna voiska*, 507, 28. 1. 1948.

42 *Razvoj Oruzanih snaga SFRJ*, 4, p.431 and Vol.3–II, p.161.

43 *Dokumenti o spoljnoj politici SFRJ, 1947*, vol. I, p.189; Janus Ledwoch, *Bulgaria 1954-1955*, (Warszawa, Wydawnictwo militaria, 2009), p.12.

44 *Cuvari naseg neba*, pp.255–256.

45 *Razvoj Oruzanih snaga SFRJ*, 4. p.432; *Cuvari naseg neba*, p.255.

46 Aleksandar Radić, 'Povratak Skoda, Češka vozila u našoj vojsci', *Specijalno izdanje magzina Odbrana, Arsenal br. 58*, (15. oktobar 2011); Šime Oštrić–Ognjan Petrović, 'Avia S–92 Turbina', *Aeroplan* (jul–avgust 1989), br. 4, 18–21; Petr Brojo, Jozef Studeny, 'The Czechoslovak army 1945–1954', (Prague: Capricorn Publications, 2012).

47 Bojan Dimitrijević, 'Stosunki wojskowe pomiedzy Jugoslawia a Polska i Czechoslowacja w latach 1945–1948', in collection of works: *Polska i Jugoslawia po II wojnie šwiatowej*, (Bydgoszcz: Uniwersytet Kazimierza Wielkiego, 2016. pp.71–80.

48 *Razvoj Oruzanih snaga SFRJ*, 10, p.66; *Narodna armija*, 23 June 1949; Živković, *Centar vojnih škola kopnene vojske*, p.99.

49 *Razvoj Oruzanih snaga SFRJ*, 3–II, p.163.

50 Kljakic, *Izgubljena pobeda Generala Markosa*, pp.281–282.

Chapter 4

1 Kardelj, *Borba za priznanje i nezavisnost nove Jugoslavije 1944-1957*, p.69.

2 Robert Lee Wolf, *The Balkans in Our Time* (New York: Norton Library, 1967), pp 354–355.

3 Wolf, *Balkans*, p.353.

4 *Razvoj Oružanih snaga SFRJ 1945–1985*, 10, pp.73–75; *Oružane Snage SFRJ*, p.224; *Razvoj Oruzanih snaga SFRJ*, 12.

5 *Bela knjiga o agresivnim postupcima* (Belgrade, 1951), p.315 and onward.

6 General–major Roglić Stevan, *Rađanje našeg RV i PVO*, Glasnik RV i PVO, 2/1972, p.27.

7 *Cuvari naseg neba*, pp.187–188.

8 AJ, A CK SKJ, Albanija, IX, 1/I, K.2/154, 155.

9 AJ, A CK SKJ, IX 1/IV–27, 3–4.

10 Kardelj, *Secanja*, p.116.

11 Kljakic, *Izgubljena pobeda Generala Markosa*, p.131.

12 Kardelj, *Secanja*, pp.116–117.

13 *Cuvari nasg neba*, p.188; Wolf, *Balkans*, p.356.

14 Kardelj, *Secanja*, pp.127–128 and 216.

15 Djodje Ličina, *Izdaja* (Zagreb: CIP, 1986), p.92.

16 Letters to editor, *Duga, illustrated magazine*, no 394/5, Belgrade 1990.

17 *Razvoj Oružanih snaga SFRJ 1945–1985*, 3–2, pp.162–163 and 272--273.

18 Ličina, *Izdaja*, pp.28–39.

19 AJ, A CK SKJ IX 1/IV–27, 68; AJ, A CK SKJ, Albanija, IX, 1/I, K.2/172–174; Pljaku, *Nasilje nad Albanskom revolucijom*, pp.68–69.

20 AJ, A CK SKJ, Albanija, IX, 1/I, K.2/169–191.

21 AJ, A CK SKJ, Albanija, IX, 1/IV–27, 83.

22 *Bela knjiga o agresivnim postupcima*.

23 YAF Museum, 'Testimony of Seargent Momir Kostic, given on 5. II 1959', in: Material for: *Bela knjiga*.

24 YAF Museum, k 30, 'History of the 116 fighter Regiment', p.8.

25 *Bela knjiga o agresivnim postupcima*, p.350.

26 *Razvoj Oružanih snaga SFRJ 1945–1985*, 4, p.432.

27 Milatović, *Pet diplomatskih misija*, pp.50, 71–72.

28 Shlomo Aloni, 'Spitfires for Israel, The 1948 Vintage', *Air Enthusiast* No 63, May–June 1996, pp.17–20; 'Spitfires over the strip', Aeroplane Monthly, October 1987, p.524; Elizer Cohen,

'Israel's best defense. The first full story of the Israeli Air Force (New York: Orion Books, 1993), pp.46–47; Israeli Defence Force Archives, series 600137/1951, file 577, mifc'a Velveta, disk 0P019B, p.7. Document courtesy by Zdenek Klima.

29 Kardelj, *Secanja*, pp.129–131.

30 Predrag J. Marković, *Beograd između Istoka i Zapada 1948–1965* (Beograd: Službeni list SRJ, 1996), pp.123–133.

31 Bojan Dimitrijević, *JNA – od Staljina do NATO pakta* (Beograd: Službeni lits SCG, 2005), pp.154–163.

32 Ličina, *Izdaja*, pp.80–88.

33 Razvoj OS SFRJ, 12, pp.78–85.

34 Author's interviews with: Colonel Bude Bosnić (at that time in the I Department of the Federal UDBA) Belgrade 31 October 1998, Vladan Bojanić (at that time head of the II Department of the Serbian UDBA), Belgrade 1995; AJ, 507, VII, k. 14/1, p.8.

35 Ivan Matović, *Arso Jovanović, Vojskovodja sa oreolom mučenika* (Belgrade: NIC Vojska, 2001), pp.186–188.

36 AJ A CK SKJ, 1/V, K.3/9–13–14–15. and K.3/8.

37 Ličina, *Izdaja*, pp.11–41; Matović, *Arso Jovanović*, pp.191; Jakšić, *Nad uspomenama* II, p.40.

38 DA MSP, PA 1948, f 89, 7, 422203 and 8, 83129.

39 Marko Lopušina, *Ubi bližnjeg svog* (Beograd: Alfa, 1997), part I, p.65.

40 AJ, ACK SKJ VIIa–kI: 'Dokumenta KK Opunomoćstva CK KPJ za JA', br. 1049, 20. 4. 1949, 18–19 and k.14/1, 1–4.

41 Author's interview with Duško Karić, (at that time with the Federal UDBA), Belgrade 1996.

42 Interview with B. Bosnić.

43 Miroslav Popović, *Udri bandu!* (Belgrade: Filip Visnjic, 1988), pp.158–159; Dragan Marković, *Istina o golom otoku*, (Belgrade, Narodna knjiga, 1987), p.97; Dragoslav Mihailović, *Goli otok* (Belgrade: Službeni glasnik, 1990).

44 This conspirative number confirmed with the personnel documents of Asen Stefanov, who left the camp in 1954. Document courtesy by Srdjan Cvetkovic.

45 Milivoje Stevanović, *U Titovim fabrikama izdajnika* (Belgrade: Kultura, 1991), p.444.

46 Stanko Opačić – Čanica, *Srbin u Hrvatskoj, kazivanje kordunaškog seljaka, ratnika, ministra, osudjenika*, edited by Milan Vesović (Belgrade: Litera, 1989), p.96.

47 *Narodna Voiska*, No. 776 22. VII 1950, No. 1010 22. XI 1951, No. 1054 6. VII 1952 and No 1055 7. VII 1952; *Narodna armia*, No. 1460 22. V 1953.

48 Mihailović, *Goli otok*, pp.74 and 172, Slavoljub Djukić, *Čovek u svom vremenu* (Belgrade: Filip Visnjic, 1989), pp.57–72; Milovan Djilas, *Druženje sa Titom* (Belgrade: autorsko izdanje, 1990), pp.94–95.

49 Filip Bajković, 'UDBA u sistemu socijalističke demokratije', *Komunist*, 1/1951, pp.57–82.

50 Aleksandar Ranković, 'Za dalje jačanje pravosudja i zakonitosti', *Vojnopolitički glasnik* (Belgrade, 6/1951).

51 *Borba*, 26 June 1952, pp.1–2; *Sluzbeni vojni list*, 1953, No. 9, p.281.

52 AJ, fond Savezno izvrsno vece (SIV) 130, f. 992, Minutes from the meeting: 29 IX 1953.

53 AJ, 130, f.992, Minutes from the meeting: 25 VI 1953, p.13.

54 Razvoj OS SFRJ, knj 12, p.75.

55 Radovan Radonjić, *Izgubljena orijentacija* (Beograd: 1985), pp.80–81. This author quotes that total of 4,153 members of army 'opted' for Cominform.

Chapter 5

1 *Oružane snage Jugoslavije 1941–1991*, p.161.

2 Razvoj OS SFRJ, 7–1, pp.79, 85, 86 and 108.

3 Razvoj OS SFRJ, 7–2, p.100.

4 Razvoj OS SFRJ, 16–1, pp.33–39 and Razvoj OS SFRJ, 7–1, p.77.

5 Jakšić, *Nad uspomenama* II, p.79.

6 'Kazivanja narodnog heroja general–pukovnika u penziji Blaža S. Jankovića: Inžinjerija JNA od 1948 do 1955'. *Narodna armija*, 29 March 1990, pp.37–38.

7 'Kazivanja', 5 April 1990, p.40 and 12 April 1990, p.40.

8 'Kazivanja', March–April 1990.

9 Bela K. Kiraly, 'The Aborted Soviet Military Plans Against Tito's Yugoslavia', in *At the Brink of War and Peace. The Tito – Stalin Split in a Historic Perspective*, editor Wayne Vucinich (New York: East European Monographs 1982), pp.273–278.

10 Pero Simić, 'Titov dnevnik', (Beograd: Večernje novosti, 2009), pp.66–89.

11 Aleksandar Životić, 'Strah ili realnost? Mogucnost sovjetske vojne intervencije u Jugoslaviji 1948–1953', *Istorija 20 veka*, (Belgrade, 1/2022), pp.107–128.

12 Laszlo Ritter, 'War in Tito's Yugoslavia? The Hungarian Army in early Cold War Soviet strategies', in: *Balkanski pakt 1953–1954*, Edited by Milan Terzić (Beograd: Medija centar, 2008), pp.251–281.

13 Bojan Dimitrijević, JNA od Staljina do NATO pakta (Beograd: Službeni list SCG, 2006); Aleksandar Životić, *Jugoslavija, Albanija i velike sile 1945–1961* (Beograd: Arhipelag, 2011); Aleksandar Životić, *Jugoslovensko–sovjetske vojne suprotnosti 1947–1957, Iskušenja savezništva* (Beograd: Arhipelag, 2015).

14 Životić, 'Strah ili realnost?', pp.116–117.

15 Životić, 'Strah ili realnost?', pp.118–119.

16 Životić, 'Strah ili realnost?', p.120, (quoted: CIA NIE, Probably Developments in Yugoslavia and Likelihood of Attack upon Yugoslavia through 1952).

17 Ledwoch, *Bulgaria 1945–1955*, pp.14–15.

18 Životić, 'Strah ili realnost?', p.125.

19 *Dokumenti 1950*, p.365; *Razvoj OS SFRJ*, 12, p.55.

20 Tasic, *Korpus narodne odbrane Jugoslavije*, pp.437–439.

21 *Pravila za vršenje službe Narodne milicije, 1. deo*, pp.93–94.

22 Razvoj OS SFRJ, 3–1, p.57; *Bela knjiga o agresivnim postupcima vlada SSSR, Poljske, Čehoslovačke, Mađarske, Rumunije, Bugarske i Albanije prema Jugoslaviji*, (Beograd, 1951), pp.40–41; More details on border incidents in: DA MSP, PA, 'granični incidenti' (Border incidents) and KNOJ magazine: *Narodna odbrana*.

23 DA MSP, PA 1948, f–86, 4, 86–239.

24 AJ, A CK SKJ, Albanija, IX, 1/I, K.2/208.

25 *Enver Hodžina Albanija* (Beograd: Tanjug, 1981), pp.135; Životić, *Jugoslavija, Albanija i velike sile*, pp.331–350.

26 *Narodna voiska*, br. 574, October 1948; Kosta Ananiev, *Vnšnoto razuznavane na Blgarija, spomeni i razmisli*, (Sofia, Kolins 5, 2008), pp.215, 229.

27 *Narodna armija*, 22 December 1949.

28 *Narodna odbrana*, broj 29, 1949. 3.

29 DA MSP, 1949, f–61, 2, 61/40–44; *Narodna odbrana*, 33, 13 August 1949; *Narodna armija*, 13 August 1949.

30 DA MSP, str. pov 1949, f–11, 8, 1145, 1149. (Border incidents for period May–June 1949) and 1949, f–60, 10–15.

31 *Narodna odbrana* 31, 30. July 1949 and 39, 24 September 1949.

32 Diplomatic Note dated on 30 August 1950 for period 15 July – 18 August 1950, with details on 10 incidents. *Dokumenti*, 1950, pp.195–196.

33 *Bela knjiga*, pp.375–376; *Enver Hodžina Albanija*, p.135; Ličina, *Izdaja*, pp.158–159; Životić, *Jugoslavija, Albanija i velike sile*, pp.331–350.

34 *Front* 44, 29 October 1949; DA SMIP, 1949, f–60, 12, 60341; 13, 60400; 14, 60427, 60474; 15, 60501, 60517, 60561 and 60562.

35 *Narodna odbrana* 3 and 5, 14 and 28 January 1950 and 36 and 37, 2, 9. September 1950.

36 AJ, 836 (Kancelarija maršala Jugoslavije), II–5–a–1/21; Tasic, *Korpus narodne odbrane Jugoslavije*, p.289.

37 *Dokumenti* 1950, pp.40–41.

38 *Dokumenti* 1950, p.159.

39 *Bilo je to na granici*, pp.20–21.

40 DA MSP, 1950, f–50, 14, s–2; 16, 413295; 17, 415716; 18, 416584; 19, 417207; 19, 41788, 417883, 417820; 21, 421086, 419464, 421408, 413004; 22, 424064; *Narodna odbrana*, 26, 24 June 1950; *Narodna odbrana* 27, 32 and 39, 1 July, 5. August and 23 September 1950; *Narodna odbrana*, 43, 21 October 1950.

41 *Narodna voiska*, 713, 28. 2. 1950 and 734, 18. 4. 1950.

42 *Za pobedu*, 151, 1 August 1951 and 189, 15 March 1953.

43 DA MSP, 1950, f–50, 14, s–2; 16, 413295; 17, 415716; 18, 416584; 19, 417207; 19, 41788, 417883, 417820; 21, 421086, 419464, 421408, 413004; 22, 424064; *Narodna odbrana*, 26, 24 June 1950; *Narodna odbrana* 27, 32 and 39, 1 July, 5. August and 23 September 1950.

44 Albanian diplomatic note dated on 10 July 1950, contains 10 violations of Albania's territory carried by the Yugoslav Army units, during June 1950. Even more, one Yugoslav soldier was wounded in the raid that occurred on 17 June 1950. *Dokumenti* 1950, pp.417–418 and 420.

45 *Bela knjiga*, pp.376–385 and 432–435.

46 DA MSP, 1951, f–46, 8–11; *Borba*, 7 April, 24 April, 16, 26 and 30 June, 15 July, 9 August, 8 September 1951.

47 Darko Bekić, *Jugoslvija u hladnom ratu* (Zagreb: Globus, 1988) p.296.

48 DA MSP, 1951, f–46, 8–11; *Borba*, April–October 1951.

49 *Narodna odbrana*, 36, 20. oktobar 1951.

50 *Za pobedu*, 124, 10 October 1950 and 159, 1 December 1951; *Narodni vojnik*, 196, 12 June 1953; *Narodna odbrana* 40, 7 October 1949, 48, 26 November 1949, 14, 1 April 1950, 23, 3 June 1950, 35, 13 October 1951; *Borba*, January to October 1951.

51 *Narodna voiska*, 1005, 1006 and 1007, 15, 16 and 17. 11. 1951.

52 *Bela knjiga*, pp.432–435.

53 *Narodna voiska*, 1008, 19.11. 1951.

54 *Narodna voiska*, 1035, 5.1. 1952.

55 *Narodna odbrana* 1–42, January to October 1952.

56 *Narodna odbrana* 3, 19 January 1952; *Borba*, March to October 1952.

57 *Borba*, March to October 1952.

58 *Za pobedu*, 178, 1 October 1952, 182, 1 December 1952; *Borba*, 19 March 1953.

59 *Narodna voiska* br. 1088–1066, March to June 1952. *Narodna armia*, January to April 1953.

60 Iordan Baev, *Sistemata ya evropeiska sigurnost I Balkanite v godinite na Studenata voina* (Sofia: izdavatelstvo Damian Iakov, 2010), p.126.

61 *Krila armije*, 196, 27 July 1952.

62 *Narodna odbrana*, 30 – 26 July 1952, 43 – 25 October 1952; 44 – 1 November1952; Borba, March to December 1952.

63 *Krila armije*, November–December 1952.

64 DA MSP, str. pov. 1952, f–15, 1, 117/9.

65 *Text of notes presenting formal diplomatic claims by the United States against the Soviet and Hungarian Governments in the case of the four American airmen and the C–47 brought down in Hungary on November 19, 1951*, DA SMIP, 1953, f–79, 4 (brochure).

66 Milatović, *Pet diplomatskih misija*, pp.115–132.

67 Author's interview with Nikola Nikolić (at that time with Intelligence Sub–centre in Senta, I Department of the Federal UDBA), Belgrade July 2017; Interview with Colonel Bude Bosnić; More details in: Milatović, *Pet diplomatskih misija*, pp.134–135.

68 Mita Miljković, *Burne diplomatske godine, iz sofijskog dnevnika 1953–1956* (Beograd: Službeni list SRJ, 1995), pp.88–94.

69 Iordan Baev, *KGB v B'lgaria, S'trudnicestvo mezdu s'vetskite I b'lgarskite taini sluzbi 1944–1991* (Sofia: Voenno izdatelstvo, 2009); Tasic, *Korpus narodne odbrane Jugoslavije*, pp.285–286.

70 Baev, *Sistemata ya evropeiska sigurnost*, p.125.

71 *Elaborat: Jugoslovenska eMiGracija u Madjarskoj*, (Beograd DSUP, UDB I Odelenje, Br IB/El.2, januar 1954).

72 *Elaborat: Jugoslovenska eMiGracija u Albaniji*, (Beograd DSUP, UDB I Odelenje, Br A/El.5 II deo, maj 1955).

73 Christopher Andrew and Vasili Mitrokhin, *The Sword and Shield, The Mitrokhin Archive and the Secret History of KGB* (New York: Basic Books, 1999), pp.355–358.

Chapter 6

1 VA, fond JNA, k.13, f. 1, 2; Aleksandar Životić, 'Zašto je reorganizovana Jugoslovenska armija 1948? Ratni plan Maksimum', *Istorija 20. veka* (Belgrade 1/2008), pp.57–70.

2 VA, fond VBA, k.14, 6.3.03.2. sveska br.16, p.16.

3 *Oružane snage SFRJ 1941–1981*, p.160; *Razvoj OS SFRJ*, 3–3, pp.513–514.

4 Bojan Dimitrijević, *Modernizacija i intervencija, Jugoslovenske oklopne jedinice 1945–2006* (Beograd: ISI, 2010). p.406.

5 *Razvoj OS SFRJ*, 3–2, pp.415–417.

6 Ministarstvo odbrane, Sektor za ljudske resurse, Uprava za organizaciju (MO, SLJR, UO): '*Knjiga mobilizacijskog razvoja JA i KNOJ–a prema naređenju 67. od 24. jula 1949*, III uprava GŠ JNA'. Numerical names of divisions were changed upon the order: str. pov. 902 dated on 20 September 1948. Titles of the armies were changed upon the order str. pov. 566 dated on 14 May 1948.

7 *Razvoj OS SFRJ*, 5, pp.67–69.

8 Museum JRV, fond RV i PVO, 'Pregled komandi, jedinica i ustanova RV i PVO sa petocifrenim i četvorocifrenim brojevima mirnodopskim vojnih pošta' (without signature).

9 VA, fond JNA, k.12, f.4, 2/1 and k.670, f.2, 5/1; MO, SLJR, UO, '*Knjiga mobilizacijskog razvoja JA i KNOJ–a prema naređenju 67. od 24. jula 1949*, III uprava GŠ JNA'.

10 Razvoj OS SFRJ, 7–1, p.85.

11 Razvoj OS SFRJ, 3–1, p.59.

12 VA, fond JNA, k. 12, f.4, 2/1, 14/1 i 15/1.

13 VA, fond JNA, k. 12, f.4, 14/1; Razvoj OS SFRJ 3–2. 164; Interview with Dušan Bilandžić, Pecs 1998.

14 VA, fond JNA, k.12, f.4, 8/1 'Naređenje za predislokaciju vazduhoplovnih jedinica od 28. septembra 1949'.

15 VA, fond JNA, k.287, f.5 1/1

16 VA, fond JNA, k.287, f.5 1/1; MJRV, fond RV i PVO, k.6–1.

17 Razvoj OS SFRJ, 3–1, 3–1, pp.64–70.

18 *Oružane snage Jugoslavije 1941–1991*, p.163.

19 VA, fond JNA, k.52, f.2, 1/1–4.

20 MO, SLJR, UO, 'Naređenja Vrhovnog komandanta': GŠ JA III uprava, pov br. 42–8. 1. 1951, pov. br 74–10. 1.1951, pov br. 150–20. 1. 1951; *Razvoj OS SFRJ*, 9–1, p.117.

21 Dušan Vukadinović – Gliso Vejnović, *Centar visokih vojnih škola JNA 'Maršal Tito'* (Beograd: VIZ, 1983), pp.85–94 and 423.; *Razvoj OS SFRJ* 7–1, p.126; 'Kazivanja narodnog heroja general-pukovnika u penziji Blaža S. Jankovića', *Narodna armija*, 29 March 1990, p.36.

22 VA fond JNA, k. 732–5, e–2; *Razvoj OS SFRJ* 10, pp.308, 332.

23 *Razvoj OS SFRJ*, 10, 103–104; For details on histories of School Centres see: *Vojni leksikon, Trideset godina Školskog centra PVO*, (Zadar 1975); *35 godina roda ABHO* (Beograd: VIZ, 1980).

24 Razvoj OS SFRJ 1945–1985, knj 10, p.331.

25 Aleksandar S. Jovanović, *Poraz, koreni poraza* (Beograd: 2001), p.287.

26 AJ, 507, A CK SKJ, II, K.4/39.

27 Potpukovnik V. Miladinovic, 'Patriotizam pripadnika naše armije', *Vojnopoliticki glasnik* (Belgrade 10/1949), pp.10–19.

28 Major Vojin Milic, 'O novom jugoslovenskom socijalistikom patriotizmu', *Vojnopoliticki glasnik* (Belgrade, 2/1949), pp.45–48.

29 *Narodna armija*, November–December 1951, May 1953 and September 1954.

30 Josip Broz Tito, *Govori i članci IV* (Zagreb: Naprijed, 1959), p.13.

31 VA, fond JNA, k. 50, f.4, 5/1 and k.288, f.3, 2–8/1.

32 *Razvoj OS SFRJ* 3–2, pp.168, 294 and 306.

33 *Borba*, 9. novembar 1950, p.1.

34 VA, fond JNA, k. 294, f.6 1/1.

35 Razvoj OS SFRJ, 5, p.61.

36 General-pukovnik u pen. Zdenko Ulepič, 'Posleratni razvoj jugoslovenskog ratnog vazduhoplovstva i protivvazdušne odbrane', *Glasnik RV i PVO*, 2/1972, p.39; For a detailed account on the atmosphere in the JRV units, see: *Zgode o obrambi neba, vrazji (slovenski) fantje v letecih strojih*, Revija Obramba, posebna izdaja (Ljubljana, Obramba, December 2010).

37 Document: 'Komanda JRV, str. pov. Z. br. 55, 17. 10. 1950. god'. (Courtesy of Čedomir Janić).

38 *Razvoj OS SFRJ*, 9–1, p.106 and 118–123.

39 *Narodna armije*, 11. 10. 1949; *Razvoj OS SFRJ*, 3–1, pp.86 and 3–2, p.168.

40 MJRV, RV i PVO, k.30, 'Istorijat 116.lap', pp.9–10.

41 J. B. Tito, *Stvaranje i razvoj Jugoslovenske armije* (Beograd: Glavna politicka uprava 1949), pp.372–386; *Front*, 94, 1949.

42 *Narodna armija*, 25. 11. 1972.

43 'Ekspoze Maršala Tita u Narodnoj skupštini o vojnom budžetu za 1951', *Vojnopolitički glasnik* 12/1950, pp.1–17; *Dokumenti 1950*, pp.359–360.

44 *Razvoj OS, SFRJ*, 9–3, pp.88–89.

45 Omer Pezo, *Vojna industrija Jugoslavije* (Belgrade: VIZ, 1983), pp.43–44; *Oružane snage Jugoslavije 1941–1981*, pp.584–585; Janić, *70 godina vazduhoplovne industrije Jugoslavije*.

46 AJ, f. 25, 4–53.

47 *Oružane snage Jugoslavije 1941–1981*, p.605.

48 Document: MNO, zamenik ministra, pov. br 267, 31. 8. 1950; *Razvoj OS SFRJ*, 7–2, pp.140–151.

49 *Borba*, 29. 3. 1952.

50 Razvoj OS SFRJ, 16, pp.136–156.

51 Razvoj OS SFRJ, 17, pp.420–422.

52 Pezo, *Vojna industrija Jugoslavije*, pp.147–148; *Razvoj OS SFRJ*, 16, pp.137–178; *Razvoj OS SFRJ*, 17, p.203; AJ, A CK SKJ, V, k–II, /1–63, 14–15.

53 VA, k.435, (GŠ 18) f.3, 1/21, 23, 66–67; Manojlo Babić, *Vrhovni komandant među tenkistima* (Beograd: VIZ, 1982), pp.79–82.

54 'Delo trudbenika vojne industrije: naš tenk', *Narodna armija*, 1 and 2. 5. 1950.

55 VA, k.435, f.3, 1/84.

56 *Razvoj OS SFRJ* 17, p.253; *Front* 94, November 1949; kapetan Miodrag Milojević, 'Naša industrija motornih vozila', *Tenkovski glasnik*, 3/1950 (Belgrade 1950), pp.58–63.

57 Janić, *70 godina vazduhoplovne industrije Jugoslavije 1923–1993*.

58 MJRV, 'Registri aviona Komande JRV and 7. vazduhoplovnog korpusa' and 'Registri motora Komande JRV'.

59 Borislav Vasić, *Avioni jugoslovenskog neba* (Beograd: 1987), pp.7–19; Zlatko Rendulić, *Avioni domaće konstrukcije posle Drugog svetskog rata* (Beograd: 1996), pp.35–48; Janić, *70 godina vazduhoplovne industrije Jugoslavije*; Nikola Žutić, *Ikarus-Ikarbus 1923–1998* (Beograd: BMG–Ikarbus, 1999), pp.38–39.

60 Milan Micevski, 'Branilac prestonice, lovacki avion Ikarus S–49A', *Arsenal br. 9, Posebno izdanje lista Odbrana*: 15 September 2007; Rendulić, *Avioni domaće konstrukcije*, pp.48–51.

61 MJRV, 'Registri aviona Komande JRV and 7. vazduhoplovnog korpusa' and 'Registri motora Komande JRV'; Milan Micevski, 'Poslednji domaci lovac, Avion Ikarus S–49C', Arsenal br.19, *Posebno izdanje lista Odbrana* 15 July 2008; Z. Rendulić *Avioni domaće konstrukcije*, pp.48–52.

62 Žutić, *Ikarus–Ikarbus 1923–1998*, pp.38, 42–43.

63 *Razvoj OS SFRJ* 16, pp.400–458.

64 Grupa autora, *Podmornicarstvo Jugoslavije* (Beohgrad-Lljublajan–Pula: Udruzenje Podmornicar, 2012), p.86; Bosko Antić, *Podmornice* (Beograd: NIU Vojska 1996), pp.98–99.

65 *Čuvar Jadrana* 179, 8. februar 1952; *Borba*, July 1952.

66 *Razvoj OS SFRJ* 5, p.52.

67 *Razvoj OS SFRJ* 5, pp.52–55; Tito, *Govori i članci*, vol. VI, pp.63–64.

Chapter 7

1 More details on political context in: Lorraine M. Lees, *Keeping Tito Afloat, The United States, Yugoslavia and the Cold* War (University Park: Penn State University Press, 1997); Beatrice Heuser, *Yugoslavia in Western Military Planning 1948–53*, in: *Yugoslavia's Security Dilemmas*, edited by Marko Milivojević, (New York: Berg, 1988), pp.126–136.

2 Leese, *Keepin Tito Afloat*, p.115; Heuser, pp.137–139.

3 Dragan Bisenić, 'Sveočenje Vladimira Velebita', *Politika* (Belgrade: 27 March 2001); Bekić, *Jugoslavija u Hladnom ratu*, p.232.

4 Bisenić, 'Sveočenje Vladimira Velebita' (27, 28 and 29 March 2001); DA MSP, PA, str. pov, 1951, f–9, 7, 1687.

5 Bekić, *Jugoslavija u Hladnom ratu*, p.318.

6 VA, JNA, k. 14, f.9, 2/1; DA MSP, PA, str. pov, 1951, f–9, 7, 1902, 2176 and 1952, f–75, 21, 417486; *Borba* 15 November 1951, pp.1–3; *Obavestajna sluzba Sjedinjenih Američkih Država*, (DSNO Uprava Bezbednosti, poverljivo, br. evidencije 5921, Beograd 1968), p.47; Bojan Dimitrijević and Milan Micevski, *JETS, avioni americkog porekla u jugoslovenskom naoruzanju 1953–1974* (Beograd: Spekltar, 1991), p.1; 'Sporazum između vlade FNRJ i vlade SAD o vojnoj pomoći od 14. 11 1951' in *Međunarodni ugovori FNRJ*, 1/1952 (Beograd, 1952), Ranko Petković, *Jedan vek odnosa Jugoslavije i SAD* (Beograd: VINC, 1992), pp.102–105.

7 Tito, *Govori i članci*, vol.VI, p.289.

8 *Borba*, 22 December 1951.

9 VA, JNA, k.21, f–3, R br.3.

10 DA MSP, 1951, f–78, 6, 'Izveštaj o pomoći u prehrambenim artiklima Jugoslaviji za savlađivanje posledica suše', DA MSP, PA str. pov. 1952, f–14, 10, 2303; AJ, SIV, 920/1400 (1954).

11 Bekić, *Jugoslavija u Hladnom ratu*, p.318; DA MSP, 1951, f–22, 19, 44830.

12 Micevski Milan and Dimitrijević Bojan, *Balkan Mosquitos*, *Flypast*, November 1990.

13 VA, JNA, k.21, f–3, R br.3.

14 Mirko Roganovic, '30 godina jedinica VOJIN', *Glasnik RV i PVO* 3/83, (Belgrade, 1983), pp 8–9.

15 *Razvoj OS SFRJ*, 5, chapter: 'Relations with the USA' and appendix 11.

16 *Razvoj OS SFRJ*, 5, appendix 6.

17 VA, JNA, k.21, f.3. 3 14; Ivan Laković, *Zapadna vojna pomoć Jugoslaviji 1951–1958* (Podgorica, 2006).

18 Wolf, *The Balkans in Our Time*, p.415.

19 VA, JNA, k.16, f.3, 1/4; *Balkanski pakt*, pp.311–313; *Borba*, 1 March 1953; Bekić, *Jugoslavija u Hladnom ratu*, pp.496–498.

20 DA MSP, str. pov 1953, f–5 'Bilten DSIP FNRJ 5/1953'.

21 *Borba*, 15–22 February 1953; VA, JNA, k.15 f.1, 1/1 and f.2, 3; *Balkanski pakt*, pp.256–309, 552–555; *Enciklopedija Jugoslavije* (Zagreb: 1955), vol. I, p.317; DA MSP, str. pov 1954, 'Bilten DSIP FNRJ 20/1953', pp.2–3.

22 Wolf, pp.416–417.

23 Bojan Dimitrijević, *Od Staljina do Atlanskog pakta – Armija u spoljnoj politici Titove Jugoslavije 1945–1958*, (Belgrade, Službeni list SCG, 2005).

24 *Borba*, 7 to 12 March 1953; DA MSP, PA, 1953, f–23, 10, 417734.

25 Tito, *Govori i clanci*, vol.8, pp 34–35 and 45–50.

26 *Borba*, 27 April 1953.

27 *Borba*, 24 and 29 January, 1, 5 and 14 March, 5, 6 and 7 May 1953.

28 *Borba*, 11 and 18 June 1953.

29 *Narodni vojnik* 196, 12 June 1953.

30 *Borba*, 5, 6 and 7 May 1953; *Za pobedu*, 199 and 202, 15. August and 1 October 1953.

31 *Borba*, 3 June 1953.

32 *Za pobedu*, 196, 1 July 1953; *Borba*, 27 and 28 June 1953.

33 *Borba*, January to October 1953.

34 DA MSP, 1953, f–47, 8, 418267 and 418268.

35 *Za pobedu*, 197, 15 July 1953; *Borba*, 8, 25 August 1953.

36 *Borba*, 15 and 16 August 1953.

37 DA MSP, 1953, f–47, 6 and 8; *Međunarodni ugovori FNRJ*, sv. 30 (Belgrade 1954) and 29/1955 (Belgrade, 1955).

38 Miljković, *Burne diplomatske godine*, pp.45 and 50.

39 VA, VBA, 'Uprava bezbednosti SSNO, Istorijski razvoj službe bezbednosti OS SFRJ', pp.50–51.

40 *Kampanja protv FNRJ 1948–1958*, (Belgrade, Uprava za MPV, Oktobar 1958), p.65.

41 Bojan Dimitrijević, 'Intelligence and Security Services in Tito's Yugoslavia 1944–1966', *Istorija 20. veka* 2–2019, (Beograd 2019), pp.9–28.

42 'Deset godina UDB–e', *Narodna milicija*, p.5; *Narodna armija*, 22 December 1954, pp.16–27.

43 DA MSP, 1951, f–46, 12.

44 DA MSP, PA 1948, f 89, 7, 422203 and 8, 83129.

45 Dimitrijević, *Jugoslovensko ratno vazduhoplovstvo 1942–1992*, pp.87–88.

46 *Mir Aviacii*, 2/1997, p.20.

47 *Narodna odbrana*, 11, 15 March 1952; *Borba*, 15 March 1952.

48 *Krila armije*, 194, 13. July 1952; *Borba*, 6–15 July 1952.

49 *Borba*, 29 September 1953.

50 *Vazduhoplovni opitni centar 1923–2003*, edited by Bojan Dimitrijević (Belgrade: VOC, 2003), p.48.

51 'US MiGs', *Air Forces Monthly*, June 2001, p.22.

52 *Razvoj OS SFRJ*, 3–1, pp.70–71 and 3–2, pp.166–168; *Oružane snage Jugoslavije 1941–1991*, p.163; *Priručnik za mornara-graničara*, p.40; VA JNA: k.19, f.1, 4/1 and k.19, f.1, 7/1. 'Analiza b/g za JRM u 1953. godini', k.91, f.4/4, k.93, f.1/24, k.116, f.1, 32/1 and 32/9, k. 93, f–4, 4/1, k. 97, f–1, 9, k. 763, pp 101 and 686 and k. 774. 1.

53 VA, VBA, k.32, 7.1.01, sveska br.2.

54 VA, JNA, k.91, f.6/1.

55 *Gardist*, 2, 25. January 1953; *Borba*, 15 January 1953, p.1.

56 VA, JNA, k.93, f.1/1.

57 *Borba*, 7 January 1953, 11 January 1953, 28 April 1953 and 15 August 1953.

58 *Borba*, 2 June 1953; Službeni vojni list 9/1 June 1953. p.268 ('Naredba MNO br. 111', 1 June 1953); Drago B. Nikolić, *Razvoj politickih organa u Jugoslovenskoj narodnoj armiji* (Beograd: VIZ 1985), pp.110–120.

59 VA, JNA, k.93, f.1/3. (Nar.pov. br.63, 17. I 1953).

ABOUT THE AUTHOR

Bojan Dimitrijevic is a historian working as Deputy Director of the Institute for Contemporary History in Belgrade, Serbia. He was educated at the universities of Belgrade and Novi Sad, CEU Budapest and the University of Bradford. In 2003–2009 he served as advisor to the Minister to the Serbian MoD, the Minister of Foreign Affairs and to the President of Serbia and as Assistant to the Minister of Defence. His research has included the military history of the former Yugoslavia, the Balkans in the Second World War, the Cold War and diverse conflicts ever since. He has published over 80 books and 130 scientific articles. This is his eighth title for Helion.